WILDLIFE GARDENS

COMPLETE GARDENER'S LIBRARY™ 5/06

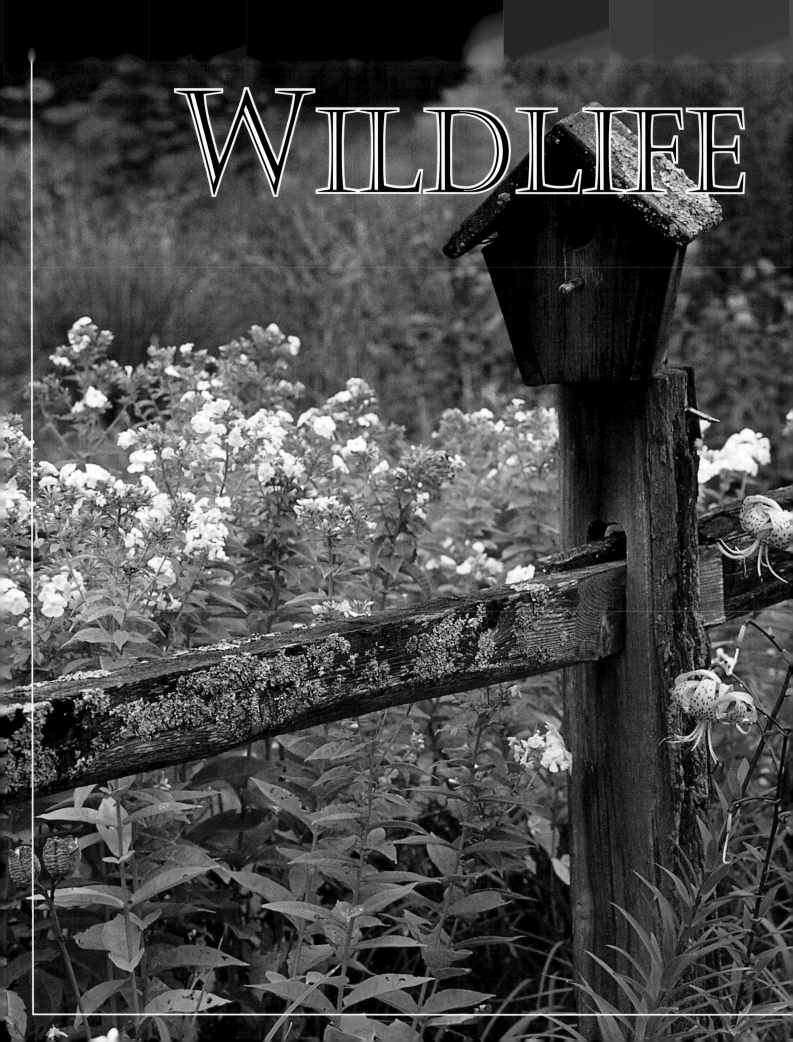

WILDLIFE

GARDENS

Katharine Anderson

with
Tom Carpenter
Justin Hancock
and Anne Price

NATIONAL HOME
GARDENING CLUB

**National Home
Gardening Club**
Minneapolis, Minnesota

WILDLIFE GARDENS

Mike Vail
Vice President, Product Marketing/Business Development

Tom Carpenter
Director of Book and New Media Development

A. Cort Sinnes
Home Gardener's Library Executive Editor

Julie Cisler
Book Design & Production

Dan Kennedy
Book Production Manager

Michele Teigen
Book Development Coordinator

Molly Rose Teuke
Justin Hancock
Copy Editor

10 9 8 7 6 5 4 3
SBN 0-914697-99-4

National Home Gardening Club
12301 Whitewater Drive
Minnetonka, Minnesota 55343

Photo Credits
William D. Adams: 6, 36 (2), 69, 118, 122, 126, 141, 145 Jim Block: 2-3, 4 (3), 5, 6 (2), 7 (3), 8, 11, 12, 14 (3), 15, 16 (2), 21 (2), 23, 25, 26 (2), 27 (3), 28 (2), 30 (2), 31, 32, 33 (2), 35 (2), 39, 41, 42 (2), 43, 44 (2), 45, 46 (4), 48 (2), 49 (3), 52, 54, 57 (2), 58, 59 (2), 62, 63, 64, 65, 68, 69, 70-71, 72, 73, 75, 81 (2), 81 (3), 83 (4), 90, 93, 94, 95 (2), 96, 97 (3), 98 (4), 99 (4), 100, 101, 108, 109, 110-111, 112-113, 114, 115, 116 (5), 117 (2), 118, 120 (2), 121 (3), 122, 123 (3), 124, 126 (4), 127, 128 (3), 129 (2), 132, 133, 135, 137, 144 (2), 146 Walter Chandoha: 24, 67, 68, 79, 96, 106, 107, 114, 120, 124, 125, 134, 136 (2), 137, 138 Rosalind Creasy: i, 92 (2), 104 James F. Dill: 46, 54, 59 Derek Fell: 10, 17, 21, 53, 55, 56 (2), 58 (2), 61, 67, 73, 75, 78, 82 (2), 89, 115, 138, 139 (2), 142-143, 144 (2), 147, 148, 149 Marge Garfield: 5, 12, 39, 48, 50-51, 55, 68, 74, 91, 98, 100, 116, 127, 129 (2), 134 Saxon Holt: 31 (3), 80 (9), 87, 88, 90, 114, 115, 145 Bill Johnson: 13, 116 Hugh Palmer: 7 Jerry Pavia: 9, 29, 31, 38, 43, 54, 73, 76, 77, 84-85, 88, 90, 101, 103 (2), 114, 117, 121, 123, 124 (4), 135 Robert Perron: 11, 12, 13 Laura Riley: 25, 27, 39 (2), 45 (5), 47, 49, 118, 138 The Stock Market: 5 (2), 9, 10, 21, 27, 28 (2), 29, 30, 32, 33, 34 (3), 35, 37, 40, 44, 52, 54, 60, 65, 94 (2), 95, 102, 119 (3), 123, 127, 128, 130-131, 139, 140 Steve Swinburne: ii-iii, 8, 14, 18-19, 21, 31, 49, 66, 86 (4), 126 (2), 129, 147 Mark Turner: 12, 15, 41, 55, 62 (2), 105, 121 (2), 136 The Wildlife Collection: Cover, 20 (4), 26 (2), 33, 36, 59, 69, 118, 125(2), 132, 137

CONTENTS

Chapter 1
Discovering the Wildlife Garden — 2
    Barbara's Garden — 8
    Thinking Habitat — 10
    Regional Focus — 12
    Diversity — 13
    Connections — 14
    Ethics — 15
    How the Book is Organized — 16

Chapter 2
Who's Out There?
What are they Looking For? — 18
    Ecoregions — 22
    The Four Main Groups — 24
    Birds — 25
    Building a Purple Martin House — 31
    Mammals — 32
    Bats, the Good Guys — 37
    Amphibians — 38
    Reptiles — 40
    Toads, the Gardener's Best Friend — 42
    Insects and Other Invertebrates — 44
    Animals as Gardeners — 47

Chapter 3
Strategies for Wildlife Gardening — 50
    1. Know What's Out There Now — 52
    2. Plan Ahead to Avoid Conflicts — 52
    3. Consider the Garden as Human Habitat too. — 53
    4. Offer Food and Shelter — 54
    5. Add Water — 55
    6. Rethink Your Lawn — 56
    7. Think Diversity — 58
    Forest: Dynamic System — 60
    Prairies and Meadows: A Delicate Balance — 61

8. Relax Neatness Standards and Let in Some Wildness 62
9. Learn About Your Ecoregion, and Think of the Garden as Part of that Larger Unit 63
Hedgerows 63
10. Add Native Plants to the Garden 64
11. Avoid Invasives 65
12. Minimize Pesticides 66
13. Protect Your Guests 66
14. Use Stone Walls, Rock Piles, Fences and Paths 67
15. Create Places to Enjoy the Garden 68

Chapter 4
Water in the Garden 70

Simple Water Sources 73
Birdbaths 74
Moving Water 75
Water in Winter 76
Ponds 77
Spoo's Bog Ponds 79
How to Put in a Bog Pond 80
Water Quality and Maintenance 81
Mosquitos and Fish 81
Larger Ponds 82
Pondside Plants 82
Plants 83

Chapter 5
The Plantings 84

Legal Considerations 87
Overall Design 90
Starting from Scratch 91
Renovating an Existing Garden 92
Evaluating Plants 93
Trees: the Center of the Garden 94
Smaller Trees 95
Shrubs 96
Flowers 98
Vines 100
Grasses 102

Groundcovers 103
Planting Patterns 104
Perennial Beds 105
Island Bed 106
Hedgerow 107
Meadow and Prairie 108
Maintaining the Wildlife Garden 110

Chapter 6
Specialty Gardens 112

Birds 114
Northeast and Midwest 116
Desert, Southwest 118
Birdfeeders and Squirrels 120
South, Southeast 121
Pacific Northwest 122
Bird Houses 123
Bird Feeders 124
Hummingbird Garden 125
Butterflies 127

Chapter 7
When Wildlife is a Problem 130

Insects 134
Squirrels at Bird Feeders 135
Damage to Plants and Gardens 136
Rabies 138
Digging and Burrowing Pests 139
Intruders in the House 140
Danger: Snakes 140

Chapter 8
Enjoying Your Backyard Habitat and Beyond 142

Learning to See 144
Beyond the Garden 148
How to Raise a Monarch 150

Resources 151
Index 153

◆ CHAPTER 1 ◆
DISCOVERING THE WILDLIFE GARDEN

Today's wildlife gardening creates a wonderful place where humans, their plants and other species can live together in harmony. Cooperation, not control, is the underlying approach and the reward is a garden filled with color, sound and movement through the seasons. Wildlife gardens are relaxed and comfortable. Oaks, saguaro cactus or prairie grasses may dominate, depending on where you live. Birds and butterflies are welcome, but so are beetles, lizards, turtles, bats and so much more.

But creating a wildlife garden is not just returning a piece of land to wilderness. Rather, a wildlife garden combines the best of gardening with ecology and our instincts about the natural world. While no one has all the answers to the challenge of making sanctuaries that bridge the cultivated and the wild, there is ever more solid experience to build on.

Nesting boxes and patches of flowers encourage birds to make their homes in your yard.

The wildlife garden is, most of all, a place to relax and recover a sense of connection with other creatures.

Gardeners all over have discovered that gardening with wildlife in mind transforms their lives in unexpected ways. Saturday morning is apt to find these gardeners out in the yard as the birds begin their morning concert or with binoculars trying to identify the newest migrating visitors.

These gardeners' lawns have shrunk, requiring much less attention and worry...energy they are happier to use building a brush pile or adding a stone wall for chipmunks to hide in or stash things in or offer lizards a place to bask. Wildlife gardeners tend not to panic if caterpillars are chewing some leaves, looking forward instead to the butterflies or moths that emerge. There is no rush to clean up all fallen leaves and branches, because birds, worms and microorganisms will slowly do the job. Many of these gardeners are in touch with other wildlife gardeners and exchange news or tips on building ponds, attracting unusual birds or dealing with competition in the vegetable garden and more. They often become interested in the fate of endangered species and work to preserve natural areas in their communities.

Wildlife gardeners are an independent, curious, adventuresome and generous group. They're in cities, towns and rural areas with gardens from window boxes to 10 acre tracts. Much of what wildlife gardeners do is experimental, and surprises are part of what makes each project fun. Giant pileated

Red squirrels, an eastern species, prefer more remote forests than their grey squirrel cousins.

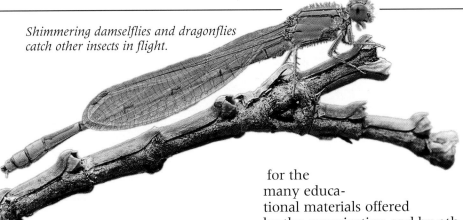

Shimmering damselflies and dragonflies catch other insects in flight.

Plan perennial beds with wildlife in mind, offering blooms from earliest spring until late fall.

woodpeckers show up unexpectedly at the bird feeder, flying squirrels paper the walls of a bluebird box with oak leaves, and the hummingbird at the beebalm turns out to be a hawkmoth.

Back in 1973, the National Wildlife Federation (NWF) started its Backyard Wildlife Habitat Program to recognize the efforts of dedicated gardeners who were providing food, shelter and water in their backyards, and to encourage others to do the same. Anyone interested in certification can apply, filling out a form that assesses the resources available to wildlife (see Chapter 3 for a sample form); those who meet the basic requirements receive an official certificate. Thousands of gardeners all over the country have received the official seal of approval, and thousands more continue to ask

for the many educational materials offered by the organization and by others who have become involved. In addition, many states have now developed programs to encourage people to garden for wildlife.

Why this growing popularity? Basically because it's so much fun and it makes us feel good. It satisfies something deep. Working with plants is therapeutic in itself; more and more studies show that humans are healthier and happier when there are trees and other green plants around them. But we humans have always loved contact with animals, too, and our senses are nourished by their presence as well. Unfortunately, in gardens, animals have too often been seen only as competitors to be kept out; the wildlife garden changes that old idea.

Humans were never meant to be separated from other animals. E.O. Wilson has recently put

forth a theory with a wonderful name: the Biophilia Hypothesis. Literally translated, it means love of life. He and others believe humans have an inborn need to relate to other life forms. Wilson says it's genetically programmed into our genes, so that to have a truly satisfying life we must somehow interact with other species. Anyone who has had a pet knows how important

Purple martins adapted centuries ago to living in homes provided by humans.

Gardens are for fun.

Big old trees are home to many creatures; small mammals and ground-dwelling birds use nearby patches of flowers and grasses to move unseen through the landscape.

such a bond can be. People also flock to zoos in incredible numbers: More people visit zoos than go to all professional sports events combined. But interactions with independent, wild-living animals are different and the good news is that you can experience them in your own yard and garden.

As you begin to look for signs of animal presence, you will hear, smell, see and feel more every day. Clues that have been there all along will suddenly become meaningful. A change in the early morning bird sounds signals the migrants are back; that spring is on its way. A flash of color in the shrubs tells where the cardinal is nesting. A whiff of rank odor means the fox passed by recently. Tracks in the snow show where the rabbits are spending the winter. The scent of blooming lilacs says it's time to look for red admiral butterflies. You will be as excited as a child when the toad comes back to the garden or when the lightning bugs come out again. Life lived with all the senses operating is what being fully human is all about.

There's a practical side to all this, too. All those animals—birds, bees, butterflies, bugs, bats, squirrels, foxes, even snakes and woodchucks—are part of a living system. The plants provide food and shelter for the animals, who in turn

Gardeners have helped bluebirds by putting up thousands of nesting boxes.

Monarch butterfly sipping from purple coneflower.

A rabbit crouches near protective brambles, considering his next move.

For spiders, fences and gates are convenient places to spin elaborate webs.

pollinate, prune, distribute, plant and fertilize the plants. So closely linked are plants and animals that some scientists have suggested that studying one without the other is absurd. This is clearly evident in the garden. We make compost heaps, but small critters do the composting. We plant tomatoes, but wouldn't have any to harvest if bees didn't pollinate them. We add organic matter to planting beds, but moles, earthworms and a host of microorganisms incorporate it into the soil. Our trees would be overrun by insects if songbirds didn't patrol them constantly. Even the much maligned snakes help with rodent control. The wildlife gardener's goal is to learn about this system and become a participant, to work with the other members of the backyard community.

Another bonus of this approach is that it means less work and more time to enjoy the garden. My friend Judy, a recent convert to the idea of wildlife gardening, called me one spring morning, to announce her delight at having new eyes for familiar scenes. She had been feeling guilty about not having cleaned out some perennial beds. But lying in her own bed that morning, she had watched red-winged blackbirds furiously scratching in the old perennials, pulling out dead leaves and dried iris stalks and flying off with them. The birds were building nests. Judy realized if she had followed the promptings of guilt and cleaned up the bed as soon as the snow melted, the birds would have missed out on some fine nesting material and Judy would have missed some fine entertainment.

Making the switch from controller to participant requires a good dose of humility and a willingness to give up some fairly entrenched ideas of how gardens are supposed to be. It isn't always easy. Neighbors (and even other family members) may object to a less-than-perfect lawn. Some animals may feel entitled to far more than their fair share of the vegetables or daylilies, and maybe even the pet food. It can take a great sense of humor and a lot of patience to work out the details of who's welcome and who isn't, and how to make that clear. Judging from the reports from committed gardeners, though, there are plenty of success stories. The process of adjustment, and the joy of gardening with wildlife in mind, inspires them to continue.

One of the joys of childhood is time spent in wild corners of the yard.

Many birds, like this song sparrow, never show up at feeders because they rely on tree-dwelling insects for food.

BARBARA'S GARDEN

I wish everyone interested in wildlife gardening could visit Barbara Nardozzi's garden in Vermont. She has gone through a remarkable change in garden style and fully appreciates how it has affected both the plantings and her whole family's life.

When I first met her many years ago, she had a beautiful walled English cottage garden that bloomed all season in perfectly-kept, color-coordinated beds. She also had a formal herb garden modeled after one at Colonial Williamsburg. The combination was her pride and joy, a real showplace that was featured in *Garden Design* magazine in 1986. No native plants for her, no plant out of place. All was carefully controlled. "I wanted England: flowers blooming all the time, planned, spilling out, profusion," she told me. "Back then my idea of wildlife in the garden included only birds and butterflies. I was a slave to that garden. It took all my time."

Today she has a backyard that is registered as an official wildlife habitat with the

Blooming lilacs signal it's time to look for red admiral butterflies.

NWF. She is an herbalist who raises plants for use in her own preparations and for classes she teaches. The new garden is beautiful, but it is also a place she and her family enjoy year-round and it provides food and shelter for them along with a whole host of other species. Best

of all, there is plenty of time to enjoy it.

When I brought a class of university students to visit there early one summer, they could hardly be persuaded to leave. They were there to study the herbs, but wrote in their field notes about how comfortable this garden felt, how native and non-native plants mixed, how easily cultivated areas blended into the surrounding vegetation. The front of the house looks like an informal cottage garden. To the side is husband Charlie's vegetable patch and coldframe. Behind, where the land slopes to the pond, are several other beds of herbs and flowers.

A huge dead tree, a snag, dominates the view from the back deck. But it is far from dead, the grubs within feeding woodpeckers and its various cavities offering home, shelter and food storage for squirrels. Except for the areas cleared for the garden beds, the rest of the land has many trees in all stages of life.

One warm spring day in May, we sat on the deck, lis-

In early spring, ruby-throated hummingbirds returning from the south eagerly seek out any and all nectar sources.

Wild patches in even a small yard can inspire safari adventures. It's all a matter of perspective.

tening to the sounds of woodpeckers drilling and birds singing, admiring the first flush of green on the many maples and other trees, watching chipmunks and squirrels, catching a glimpse of a tufted titmouse and later the great blue heron that frequents the pond. Barbara was telling me how this garden came to be.

When she and her husband Charlie, a horticulturist, moved here eight years ago, they had great plans. Under the trees were to be terraced gardens of Virginia bluebells, azaleas and rhododendrons. It never happened. Instead they began to cooperate with what was already there. Ferns have filled in under the trees; a mass of phlox provides color. Instead of planting, they often wait to see what shows up. Barbara wanted some elderberries, and one year two popped up by the driveway, no doubt planted by birds who now enjoy the fruits in mid-summer. (Barbara harvests only about half to make jellies and other treats.)

Sections of the lawn have been turning to moss, a welcome change because it means less mowing.

"The setting helped me out," she said, "by letting me know what it was capable of. It was also a case of me opening up. There's a leap that happens. It's a sharing. I always thought of small wildlife—butterflies, pollinators, hummingbirds. I wanted wildlife, but I wanted it on my own terms. There's been a natural progression. Now I embrace it all. We have a lot of frogs, garter snakes, toads. Last year there were a lot of Japanese beetles, then I noticed the skunks eating the grubs."

There have been some compromises. "It's amazing, but the rabbits and raccoons don't touch stuff in the garden. But chipmunks have nibbled on potatoes in the ground, and they ruined one crop. We can't grow corn, partly because it's too shady, and also because of the raccoons. It's not worth it. One year the rabbits did nibble a young *Viburnum opulus* planted by the house. They gave it a haircut, all those neat

little bite marks." So now it's protected by a small wire fence.

"Nature has been my teacher all my life. But I also appreciate what human hands can do," she says. Sometimes she still misses all those flowers, and she is planning a trip to England soon to enjoy the gardens there. But she'd never give up what she has now. Her garden's fruits are much more than herbs and vegetables, and include the sight of a fox glimpsed at the water's edge, peepers welcoming spring, drifts of phlox brightening the woodland scene, chipmunks and birds on the porch feeder in coldest winter, tracks of small rodents all over the yard when the snow melts, the sound of the osprey diving for fish when he returns each year on Earth Day on his journey north.

Barbara's advice to other gardeners is to lighten up on standards. Manicured, perfectly tidy gardens have no room for anything but the plants. "Consider the notion of sharing and compromise," she says. It is this stepping outside our own concerns that is the rewarding and satisfying part of wildlife gardening.

The many layers and textures of this garden welcome a wide range of bird species, who can move around safely quite near the sitting area.

THINKING HABITAT

The biggest shift in wildlife gardening is thinking of the garden as habitat. The word habitat originally meant the life needs of a species—what it needed to live and reproduce. Within a forest, for instance, there might be habitat for squirrels, along with birds, bears, frogs, insects and others, each finding its own particular combination of plants (for food and shelter) and water (in streams, pools or damp places).

Habitat has another meaning: A particular combination of plants, such as a woodland habitat, a meadow habitat and so forth, each with its own characteristic set of plants and animals. Habitat gardening means deliberately creating such plant associations.

I use the word in both senses in this book. But I want to emphasize the older meaning, because it points out an important aspect of wildlife gardening. Animals, like humans, are

It's always thrilling to see an owl in the backyard; this is a great grey owl.

adaptable. Many have found their life needs can be taken care of within the human-created environment. A chimney swift's habitat includes chimneys for nesting. House wrens can make just about anything, including shorts hanging on a clothes line, into part of their habitat. Plenty of birds, including bluebirds and purple martins, have become so accustomed to living with humans that their "natural" habitat may be said to include nesting boxes and nearby homes.

There are good reasons to focus on making plant communities as similar as possible to those in the wild, but wildlife gardening is about more than this. Almost anything can and does become part of the habitat of some wild-living animal. Wildlife gardening explores pos-

Habitat gardening means seeing expanding our notion of home to include other species.

Native plants are best for wildlife: goldenrod feeds a whole host of insects, including many butterflies; hummingbirds love jewelweed.

sibilities in the garden setting, and the setting includes humans.

The challenge and fun of thinking habitat is learning to see from the animals' point of view. This means finding out about their life cycles—where they spend each season, what their reproductive cycles are, what they need to eat, where they find water. Unlike the usual gardening season that tends to wind down when it gets too hot or cold or dry for the familiar edible and ornamental plants, the wildlife garden's season never ends. For instance, in Vermont this means filling the bird feeders and watching the familiar chickadees, nuthatches and house sparrows in winter. I have watched a brilliant red cardinal, puffed up way beyond his usual size, sheltering among the protective, unpruned branches of a tangled shrub during a fierce snow storm. After an unseasonable late spring storm hid most food sources under a thick blanket of snow, the redwinged blackbirds came to feast on the red candles of sumac berries, left over from the year before and ignored until then. What had been attractive shrubs for me were crucial shelter and food for wildlife.

A brilliantly colored mixture of perennials in full sun attracts butterflies and hummingbirds; different animals inhabit the shady area behind.

REGIONAL FOCUS

The cool, moist climate of the Pacific northwest is perfect for a woodland garden of ferns, rhododendrons and Japanese maple.

Barbara Nardozzi's garden in Vermont has the essential ingredients for wildlife habitat: nearby water, sunny and shady areas, flowers to attract insects, plenty of cover and trees in all stages of growth, including a magnificent snag in the center.

At their best, wildlife gardens reflect their regions. A wildlife garden in the desert around Tucson, Arizona, should look nothing like Barbara's in Vermont. Geography plays a crucial role in knowing what is appropriate to any one garden, and what kinds of communities and plants might have been there earlier. For instance, what are the native plants that fed wildlife before exotic ornamentals came on the scene? The trees of the northwestern coniferous forests are not like those of the sunny southwest, and different animals depend on each. Gardening as practiced in the late 20th century has often managed to blur regional differences. Images in magazines, and plants sold in large nurseries often imply that you can grow anything anywhere. Fortunately, wildlife gardening focuses us back on native plants. Local animals are the first to appreciate this change.

In the northeast, deciduous temperate trees and perennial flower beds dominate this garden.

A Florida garden includes palmetto and other native species adapted to the hot, moist climate.

DIVERSITY

Edges and layers of habitat—from clear areas to grass to short and tall flowers, shrubs, younger trees and then mature trees—offer the diversity wildlife needs to thrive.

One of ecology's surprising insights is that the highest diversity of wildlife is not necessarily in pristine environments undisturbed by humans. In fact, areas that have been altered, especially edges between different kinds of ecosystems, harbor the greatest variety of animals and plants. The gardener who wants to attract a wide range of wildlife therefore focuses on creating a highly varied setting.

One way to do that is to include many different species of plants instead of a solid mass of one, and include different growth habits, sizes and flowering patterns. Another way is to create areas of woodland and meadow, with lots of edges between the two. This is possible even in a small yard.

Water is an essential ingredient; so are open, drier areas.

Microclimates created by north and south facing walls add to diversity, as do a variety of surface materials used on walks and patios. You can allow diversity to happen, if you are willing to let plants come in on

American toads often find their way into gardens, where they eat large quantities of insects.

their own. That's how England's celebrated hedgerows, with their rich diversity of animals and plants, developed.

Diversity also means tolerance, if not affection, for a wide variety of animal species that often don't make the "most popular" list.

CONNECTIONS

A small pond planned for wildlife features rock edges for shelter, flowers to attract butterflies, a small waterfall and shallow places for birds to bathe.

Everything a bird could want: food, water and places to perch in nearby trees.

Another lesson from ecology is that of connections. Ecosystems are often described as webs, with all creatures and processes relating to each other in complex patterns. Changes in one affect all the rest. This principle applies at all levels, from the tiny pocket garden in a city to huge nature reserves.

Early morning dew makes an elaborate spider web glisten.

Barbara noticed that the skunks had come to eat Japanese beetle grubs. Had she sprayed the beetles on first sight, that would have interrupted not only that connection with the skunk but other insect-driven cycles. Insecticides and other pesticides have little role in the wildlife garden except for occasional, targeted uses.

Connections don't stop at the property line. Wild-living creatures know nothing of these arbitrary human boundaries. Birds fly miles and carry seeds to distant places—so what is planted in your yard can have effects far away. Pesticides sprayed in one yard can drift to another, and contaminated water can poison frogs and fish downstream. It isn't necessary to know all the details of these intricate systems; being aware that anything done in one yard can have far-reaching consequences is usually enough.

On the positive side, even the smallest gardens are part of the larger network of forests, meadows, disturbed areas, successional fields, wetlands and deserts that make up the home territories of wild-living animals. Everything in the backyard is potential food or home for some wild creature, and much of this habitat is critical. Suburban neighborhoods, planted with a variety of shade trees, have become an important home for many birds and squirrels. Small pockets of fruiting shrubs can provide nesting places and welcome food for migrating birds in fall. Even the tiniest wetlands are sufficient for some species of frogs and toads to survive.

All life stages of trees provide food and shelter for wildlife, from seedlings through decaying stumps.

ETHICS

A West Virginia garden blends gracefully with the surrounding environment.

Wildlife gardening is about building relationships. Not surprisingly, there are some gray areas about how to interact with wild animals. Humans are used to being in charge of their environment, to making the rules. In interactions with other species, we have an unfortunate tendency to either get rid of them, or to treat them like pets and domesticate them. The latter seems harmless, but it can be damaging to both individuals and whole populations.

Wild animals are not pets. They should not be touched with but a few exceptions and they should not be brought from the wild to live in the garden. The reasons are many.

Some are practical—some animals carry diseases that could harm humans, some bite if they believe themselves threatened. This can go the other way as well: animals can acquire diseases that then spread to others in the wild populations. But overriding all of these is the notion of respect. If the goal is to come to some kind of understanding with other species, learning to coexist peacefully, then respect must be the first rule. That means providing as much as we choose to in the way of plants, food and water sources, then leaving wildlife to get on with its life as much as possible.

It also means that when we have invited animals to share our gardens, they must be kept safe from predation by pets. Pets, unlike wild animals, are part of the human household. They are not natural predators.

Inevitably, wildlife gardeners occasionally observe animals that are hurt, or youngsters who have fallen from the nest or been left orphaned.

Replacing a young bird in its nest is fine, but what about taking it in and raising it? Naturalists and others disagree on this question. Friends of mine in Louisiana argue about this in their home. The husband, a naturalist, believes in letting orphaned critters die if necessary, that human interference is inappropriate. His wife is trained in wildlife rehabilitation. I have seen her in spring caring for tiny naked opossum babies along with a couple of young raccoons and assorted birds. She releases them all eventually and her husband, in spite of his objections, almost always helps in their care. This is not something home gardeners should do on their own, however. There is no clear cut answer on the correct way to deal with these confusing situations. But if you do decide to intervene, seek someone who is trained to care for an injured or abandoned animal.

Some birds are thoroughly at home with people. Here's a phoebe nest on top of a porch light.

HOW THE BOOK IS ORGANIZED

Chapter 2 introduces the main characters likely to share garden space and how they vary depending on your region. The notion of ecoregions presented there is a new way of dividing up the country based on many environmental features, not just temperature zones. The rest of the chapter will focus on how to look at the garden from the creatures' point of view, and to gain some insight into their role in the dynamic life of the garden.

Chapter 3 presents the main strategies of wildlife gardening, the ways gardeners are shifting to this more inclusive way of gardening. You can pick and choose from these techniques and approaches, incorporating a few at a time, experimenting to see what works in your garden. As I hope you will see from the photographs and illustrations, and from the experiences described in the text, each garden is different, the product of a particular person, place and sequence of events. There is no one ideal to achieve. Just take an approach and see where it leads. Discovery is part of the process.

Chapter 4 deals with a specialized aspect of wildlife gardening: adding water to the garden. It is hard to overemphasize how much diversity a pool, pond or wetland garden can add to your backyard wildlife garden. So many wetlands have been destroyed all over the country that these small pools are not only fun to have for the diversity of creatures they attract, but can be crucial elements for maintaining endangered populations of water lovers like reptiles, amphibians and insects.

Choosing and arranging

Comfortable chairs invite people to slow down and wait for wildlife visitors.

plants is the topic of Chapter 5 and will help whether you are starting from scratch or modifying an existing garden. The next chapter covers specialty gardens—those plantings designated for a specific group of animals such as butterflies, birds or pollinators. Some kinds of wildlife can be a nuisance or even dangerous—how to recognize and then solve such potential problems is covered in Chapter 7. Finally, the last chapter gives suggestions for how to fully enjoy the wildlife in your garden, to learn more about it and perhaps meet other gardeners concerned about conservation issues. References to recommended books and field guides and a list of organizations in the appendix will help you find more specific information for your garden.

The information comes from experts on the subject, from wildlife guides and from other gardeners who have been experimenting with this kind of gardening all over the country. Their ideas are throughout this book.

Cedar waxwings, among the most elegant of birds, love fruit trees.

◀ CHAPTER 2 ▶

WHO'S OUT THERE?
WHAT ARE THEY
LOOKING FOR?

Hummingbirds are a perfect example of the broad connections that comprise the wildlife garden's web of life. To start, hummingbirds make their nests out of tiny bits of moss, bud scales, plant down, dandelion fluff and spent flowers of clematis or other flowers. They glue it all to branches with spider webs. That's home for the minuscule hatchlings.

As adult birds zoom from flower to flower, they use their elaborate, forked tongue to slurp up nectar and many small insects. Stuck to the birds' foreheads are tiny grains of pollen they will transfer to the next flower, ensuring pollination there. Fruits and seeds that develop will later feed bird or mammal visitors, which will distribute the seeds to ensure the next plant generation.

Searching for life in the frog pond brings a whole new dimension to the garden.

A tiny Anna's hummingbird nest, made of feathers, leaves, lichen, moss and plant down, is nearly invisible among tree twigs.

A broad-tailed hummingbird incubates its eggs.

For such tiny birds, hummers are amazingly brave, well-traveled and independent creatures. They fiercely defend all food sources, be they flowers or feeders. The same tiny birds, glimpsed briefly in northern gardens, migrate south for the winter singly, at night, all the way to the Yucatan peninsula of Mexico. Many stop over on the U.S. Gulf Coast, where thousands of bird-lovers welcome them. The birds feed voraciously on the many plants and feeders put out for for them, then cross the Gulf—a non-stop flight of more than 500 miles. When they return in spring, the hummingbirds follow a nectar trail, counting on flowers along their route to sustain them on a trip that can be several thousand miles. Unfortunately, development has altered many wild areas, often destroying the tiny birds' food sources.

Birds, flowers, pollen, leaves, trees, spiders, insects, gardens, humans, tropical and temper-

Baby hummers thrive on a high-protein insect diet.

Two young broad-tailed hummingbirds crowd their nest.

Who's watching whom?

Butterfly bush is one of the most reliable plants for attracting butterflies of all kinds.

When people plant shade trees in towns and villages, grey squirrels quickly move in.

ate areas—all are part of the network of the hummingbird's life. Anyone who feeds hummingbirds or plants flowers for their benefit is stepping into this vast web. So are gardeners who make sure there are lichens, mosses and plant down available for hummingbird nests, and abundant insects to feed them.

Hummingbirds are lucky. People like them because they are beautiful and colorful. Whole books and dozens of

Frogs and toads must return to water to lay their eggs.

magazine articles have been devoted to plantings of flowers they like. Animals such as toads, snakes and spiders, on the other hand, have not fared so well. Yet a well-functioning wildlife garden needs a variety of animals, many of which are of great help to the gardener either directly or indirectly. If you can't love them all, at least learn to let them live in peace.

Animals can be divided into four distinct groups: birds, mammals, amphibians and reptiles, and invertebrates (insects). Each group is found almost everywhere on the continent, though their numbers vary. There is no need to know all their names, nor even to see them all. But once

you realize there is a whole system of interdependent lives out there, it changes how you treat the individual inhabitants. Instead of seeing them all as threats to a pristine garden, it is easier to accept them as potential allies and to be more tolerant about sharing some of your garden's bounty.

While slurping up nectar, hummingbirds also consume many small insects.

ECOREGIONS

Which wildlife is likely to show up in your garden depends first on geography. Gardeners are used to thinking in terms of hardiness zones—areas defined by lines that connect places with minimum winter temperatures. That works fine for figuring out how far north a particular plant will thrive in a garden. But for wildlife gardening, because it's about whole communities of plants and animals, a different system is needed.

Below is a map of the United States developed by Robert G. Bailey, a geographer with the U.S. Forest Service. This map divides the country into ecoregions based on climate and vegetation.

The map shows six broad divisions. Within these are nested many more variations. As you begin wildlife gardening, it is worth locating yourself within one of these regions and getting to know more about the ecoregion you

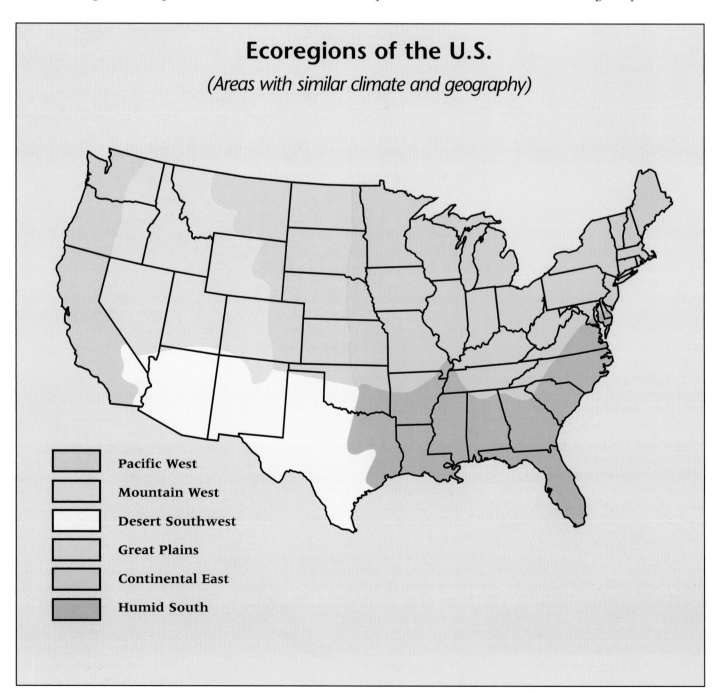

Ecoregions of the U.S.
(Areas with similar climate and geography)

- Pacific West
- Mountain West
- Desert Southwest
- Great Plains
- Continental East
- Humid South

Song sparrow on June pink azalea.

inhabit. Instead of thinking of the limits imposed by a short frost-free season or summer's excessive heat, consider that each of these regions is unique in the world and each has its own characteristics to be celebrated. In fact, each ecoregion supports its own specialized plants and animals, some of which are found nowhere else on earth.

Changing Scenes

Humans can alter ecoregions. Even Native Americans managed the land for wildlife, long before Europeans set foot in North America. The California oak woodlands—rich in deer, bear and other game—were kept that way by controlled, periodic burning. The same was true for portions of the eastern woodlands, as well as the vast prairie. Relationships with some animals were already well-developed—purple martins have been lured to live in hollow gourds placed near human habitations for century.

Europeans brought many new species of plants and animals to North America. Some were domesticated food sources, some ornamental plants and some weeds that follow humans everywhere. It is almost impossible to find areas today without some evidence of these introductions, which include starlings, house sparrows, Queen Anne's lace and Norway maples.

Wildlife Adapts

Meanwhile, native animals have adapted to living with humans. Many birds are happy to nest near homes. Some native mammals, like the raccoon and deer, have adapted so well they've become troublesome pests.

Adjustments keep changing distribution patterns. Armadillos are moving east; many birds are responding to bird feeders by extending their winter range south, or even skipping migration altogether.

But development's pace has stepped up. People are taking up more and more space, expelling animals from their homelands; some are unable to adapt. The red cockaded woodpecker of the southeast can no longer find the proper longleaf pines in which to nest, and the bird may become extinct. Black-footed ferrets of the west are declining as their main prey, prairie dogs, are eliminated for agricultural purposes.

Gardeners Care

Gardeners have played a role in helping many endangered species survive. Thousands of bluebird nesting boxes have made a real difference to that species, for instance.

City dwellers need not feel excluded from wildlife gardening. It's surprising how many species manage to survive in urban areas, reproducing and living in pockets of green like cemeteries, parks and vacant lots. The variety of wildlife in a small urban garden may be less, and their size may be smaller, but their presence brings all that much more pleasure.

Urban green places friendly to wildlife are more than refuges for the animals; these places tend to draw human neighbors, especially children, as well. By keeping alive some level of interaction with animals and demonstrating the possibilities, urban gardens may do as much to help other people as do rural or even suburban gardens. All gardens are part of the ecoregion.

THE FOUR MAIN GROUPS

One secret to successful wildlife gardening, and what makes it such fun, is trying to imagine the world from other species' point of view. Hunters do that. Native people in many parts of the world do it too. When you depend on other species, you get to know their ways very well. Animals have different ways of knowing the world—through scent, feel, powerful vision or a combination thereof—and have different requirements for comfort and safety. Keep this in mind while making gardening decisions; it will give you a new understanding of familiar, everyday scenes and objects and help you keep wildlife in your garden.

White-tailed deer, once scarce, are now considered pests in some suburban neighborhoods.

BIRDS

Birds assess the suitability of a potential home much as people assess real estate. Will I feel safe here? Does it feel and look right (not the house style, but the tree species and their arrangement)? How far do I have to go to find food? What about water? What goes on in the neighborhood (pesky neighbors or even dangerous ones, high traffic areas, noise levels)? Each species has its own notions of what makes a good home.

An important difference from people, though, is that birds look at all this from the air. They can move easily over relatively long distances, horizontally and vertically. Their eyesight is the best in the whole animal kingdom. Some birds of prey can spot their quarry a mile away; smaller birds keep constant watch for potential distant predators while searching for food close at hand. Birds learn to recognize feeders and spot them quickly. Owls see 100 times as well as humans in

Black-capped chickadee.

the dark and also have huge ear drums that help them locate even tiny movements of potential prey. Their feathers are designed for silent flight.

Each bird has its own way of moving around. Small birds can flit about in dense tangles, while some larger species have enormous wingspans that allow them to soar. Hummingbirds can hover and even fly backward.

Birdfeeding is one of the most popular backyard activities in the United States. As a result there are some birds familiar to almost everyone: chickadees, cardinals, nuthatches, downy woodpeckers, sparrows and finches.

But many birds don't eat seeds, and even those that do often rely on fruits, insects and other sources for a portion of their nutrition. To attract these birds, it takes a more indirect approach, making sure there are other reasons to visit or settle in your garden: food, water, shelter, a place to raise a family.

For instance, my friend David, an avid naturalist and birdwatcher, doesn't feed the birds at all any more, yet he has an

White-breasted nuthatches eat both seeds and insects.

The best way to attract yellow warblers is to make sure there are plenty of insects available for food.

Male northern cardinal.

Stellar jay, western relative of the blue jay.

abundance of birds on his property because they find what they need there.

Most common of the garden birds are those that belong to the passerine or perching group. These are the familiar songbirds, many of them common at bird feeders. Their feet are specially adapted for perching—three toes face forward, the other backward, for a firm grip on twig, branch or bark. Most of them migrate each year; their comings and goings mark the changing seasons.

Cardinals, tanagers, bluebirds and goldfinches flash brilliant colors in the garden, while others are better known for their songs, including the shy warblers and skilled mockingbirds.

The crow family, which includes the jays, is thought to be the most intelligent bird group. But they can also be the most infuriating—pulling up corn seedlings, calling loudly at all times of day and harassing other birds.

Finches, the largest North American bird family, are identifiable by their bulky beaks, specialized for eating seeds. Many finches are familiar because they frequent birdfeeders—among them cardinals, various kinds of grosbeaks, buntings (indigo, painted and Lazuli), purple

finches, goldfinches and crossbills. House finches, brown and white birds with deep rose or raspberry heads and breasts, are often mistaken for the purple finches in the east. They are natives of the southwestern U.S., but are spreading widely after being brought to Long Island as cagebirds, then escaping.

Warblers are the second largest bird family. There are at least 56 North American species of these small, restless birds with thin beaks. Their plumage, which can be bright yellow to dull brown, is often different in spring and fall. This, combined with their quick movements and secretive ways, makes them difficult to identify. Usually it is their beautiful songs that make warblers' presence known. They are strictly insect eaters, and are seldom spotted near feeders.

Members of the titmouse family are much easier to recognize. They include the friendly and

Rose-breasted grosbeak, a member of the seed-eating finch family.

Swallows are great insect control agents.

Robins are ground feeders.

familiar little chickadee that is often the first visitor to bird feeders and stays all winter in the North. You'll find black-capped chickadees in most of the U.S., but the Carolina chickadee inhabits areas of the southeast. Close relatives are the elegant tufted titmouse, the tiny bushtits of the western deserts and mountains and verdins of the southwest.

Often traveling in company with chickadees are nuthatches, distinctive for their peculiar way of creeping head down along tree trunks and branches as they search for insects and insect eggs.

Swallows and martins, which spend most of their time in the air swooping around for insects, have adapted well to life with people and are a common sight around homes and barns.

Also intimately tied to people are two members of the thrush family, the bluebird and robin. The much smaller hermit thrush has one of the most appreciated of all bird songs.

Wrens, another group, are so comfortable with people they will nest right above doorways or even on laundry hung on the line to dry. Though not known for feathered beauty, they are energetic, cheerful and loyal visitors who will come back to a nesting spot year after year. Cactus wrens nest within the safety of cactus thorns in the southwestern desert.

Waxwings are among the most popular and beautiful garden birds. Only two species live in North America, the cedar waxwing and the Bohemian waxwing. Both are social birds

Cactus wrens nest within protective, spiny plants.

Eastern bluebirds prefer to nest near people.

Young robin begging for food; it's fine to replace a fallen baby in its nest, but a bird this size is best left to its parents' care.

The handsome cedar waxwing, a fruit eater.

Barred owl, raptor of the night.

that travel in flocks, arriving unexpectedly to feed on favored berries and departing just as suddenly. Occasionally, a flock will stay for a few weeks as it works a preferred food source.

I was happy to see a flock one spring evening on an apple tree in bloom. The birds flitted about busily, pecking at the blossoms and passing treats of buds, petals and insects to their mates. Of all the garden birds, waxwings are probably the most dependent on fruits and berries. Orchards are one of their preferred habitats, along with woodland thickets.

Tanagers are also a treat to have in the garden because of their flashy colors. Tanagers are primarily tropical birds, but a few species make it into U.S. gardens. The male scarlet tanager is a great singer, and resplendent in its outrageously red feathers with black wings.

Mockingbirds, brown thrashers and catbirds are known for their ability to mimic the songs of other birds, and the mocking-

Scarlet tanager.

bird is the state bird for five states.

The highly specialized woodpecker family includes small downy woodpeckers, large pileated woodpeckers and various flickers, sapsuckers and others. These birds have heads built solidly to withstand the shock of hammering with their bills. Most woodpeckers listen for insects under a tree's bark, then drill into the wood or rip it apart to get the meal. The larger woodpeckers leave huge gashes that later become homes for other animals seeking shelters.

Woodpeckers also drum as part of territorial announcements, or to attract mates; sometimes they choose metal roofs for this purpose. Sapsuckers drill neat rows of holes in trees from which sap leaks, returning later to feast on insects attracted to the sap. Other birds (including hummingbirds) and butterflies also seek out these feeding spots. Pileated woodpeckers, once a rare sight except in old forests, are becoming much more common in urban areas and even show up at feeders occasionally.

Hawks and owls are raptors, or birds of prey, that feed on other animals—mammals, birds, reptiles and amphibians. Raptors are not as common in gardens as the smaller songbirds, but if trees and prey are available, some owls may take up residence.

Barn owls have long been comfortable in barns, feeding on plentiful rodents. Great horned owls are fairly common in tree-filled suburbs and even cities. Hawks generally won't nest near people, but will patrol for food in open areas. The kestrel, a small

Woodpecker stashing nuts.

hawk, sometimes swoops down onto songbirds at feeders. Because of the rapid rate of destruction of native habitats, and their need for large areas for hunting, many raptors are having to adapt to modern land uses.

Less popular in home gardens are starlings and house sparrows, both European species that tend to be greedy and noisy and crowd out other species. These introduced birds do best in densely settled areas, since they are highly adaptable and able to find food and nest sites in areas other species find inhospitable. But in some urban areas, these immigrants are the only bird life to watch, and are therefore welcomed along with the pigeons.

Food

Searching for food consumes much of a bird's attention. Their bills give clues about their diet.

Hummingbirds have bills to match the length of tubular flowers so they can reach the nectar deep within (although they also sip from other flowers).

Seed eaters have bills designed to extract or crack open seeds; cardinals, chickadees and grosbeaks can manage sunflower seeds, while goldfinches prefer much smaller ones like those of thistles. A few beaks are highly specialized. Different species of

crossbills are adapted for cracking specific pine, spruce or fir cones.

Fruits are another important food for many birds. Again, size matters. Smaller fruits, like those of many shrubs—including elderberries, blueberries, grapes and viburnums—can be easily carried off or gobbled in one bite.

Fall is important for migrating birds, who will fatten up on the abundant seed and fruit harvest in preparation for migrating. In spring, when food is scarce, some birds also rip off the succulent buds of trees and shrubs.

Important as plant foods are, many birds rely largely on animal foods for nutrition. Chickadees and nuthatches are on constant bug patrol among the trees, nabbing anything that moves on trunk, branch or leaf. During breeding season birds content with seeds in the winter change to a high-protein diet based on insects to raise their babies.

Other birds feed almost entirely on insects and other animals. Woodpeckers have tough, long bills to hammer and extract grubs, eggs and other treats in dead wood. Warblers, by contrast, have delicate, thin bills they use for nabbing smaller insects. Their long migrations in winter are necessary to find insects. The roadrunner of the southwest is a sturdy bird with a relatively long beak that devours lizards. Raptors' bills are short and have a sharp point, useful for killing and tearing apart larger animals like rodents and reptiles.

Birds feed at different levels in the canopy of trees as well as on the ground, which allows many different species to inhabit one area. Nuthatches patrol the trunk and branches, while

In their search for food, pileated woodpeckers make deep holes in trees; other animals use these holes as nests.

chickadees check the leaves for insects.

Woodpeckers and flickers specialize on getting into the wood, while towhees scratch furiously among leaves on the ground. Owls swoop down on unsuspecting rodents or other small mammals at night, hawks take over during the day. Grosbeaks, cardinals and finches take seeds; waxwings eat fruits.

Shelter

Birds need shelter for many reasons: to hide from predators, to stay warm and dry during storms and cold snaps, to eat in safety, to preen (essential care that keeps feathers in shape for flying), to search for food and for courtship. Birds look for certain kinds of places to perch. Predators like hawks choose tall trees, often isolated or dead, that give them a good view over a large area. Any birds that wants to stay safe from raptors need places to hide from danger above that are also dense enough to keep the larger birds from penetrating.

Young snowy owl.

Conifers are favorite places for many species to sit with fluffed feathers during snowstorms, because it is much warmer and less windy within. Some birds prefer to perch on open-branched trees when singing, while others consider the interior of a tangled mass of vines and shrubs as the coziest place to spend time. Cover is a key to attracting birds of all types. Carefully groomed, open landscapes are not as attractive because there is no way to hide.

Red-breasted nuthatches are familiar year-round residents in northern gardens.

Nesting

When some friends found a northern oriole nest that had fallen to the ground one spring, we spent a lot of time admiring its construction and wondering what it would be like to be a baby oriole within. Orioles weave hanging baskets of plant fibers, grasses, bark and hair, open at the top and reinforced on the bottom. Orioles suspend these basket nests from the outer drooping branches of tall trees to make an airy, swaying cradle safe from predators. The oriole's is among the most elaborate nest; other birds that follow this pattern are vireos, some warblers and the golden-crowned kinglet.

Birds are highly specific about where and how they build their nests. Each species has definite patterns. Nests may be cup shaped, shallow or deep. They can made from everything from lichens, mosses and bud scales to leaves, stalks, twigs, rootlets, fern fronds, bark, grasses, cottonwood down, straw, sheep wool, rabbit fur, cattle hair, weed stalks, cotton, rags, string and paper. Some nests even incorporate snake skins, spider cocoons and webs, or sport an exterior decorated with lichens. Mud adds strength to nests of swifts and other birds.

Where birds put their nests is often predictable, too. Cardinals, for instance, like bushes or stumps covered with a dense tangle of vines, or trees or shrubs in the border between woodlands and fields. Cardinals generally nest fairly low and they like being near people. Black-capped chickadees prefer a cavity in an old tree or a decaying stump to which they add cottony plant fibers, hairs, wool, moss and leaves and often a lining of soft plant down, wool or feathers.

Other birds make elaborate nests in sturdy locations where branches meet trunk, in thickets or among dried grasses on the ground. Conifers, deciduous trees, cacti...all have different characteristics that appeal to certain birds who look for certain heights, light conditions, protection or food availability.

Woodpeckers, flickers and sapsuckers form an important link for many other creatures by tearing holes in trees; these holes then become homes for a wide variety of other birds and mammals. Because fewer and fewer dead trees are left standing these days, some species have learned to adapt to nesting boxes built by people.

Bluebirds now nest in boxes made by people. Generations of

Northern oriole.

Each bird species has its own preferred nesting sites.

Dove nesting in cactus.

bluebirds have been brought up in these nest boxes. Now when bluebirds return in spring, they look for boxes—not trees or fence posts!

Water

Water is essential for life. Birds drink it, wash in it and use it for making mud when building nests. Birds will fly some distance to find water, but are likely to stay near a place where they can find water reliably. Swallows will dip their bills into swimming pools as they fly over for a quick drink. Puddles, small ponds, fountains and creeks are popular with thirsty birds or those wishing to bathe. A reliable water supply is one of best bird attractants you can invest in (see Chapter 4).

Mallard ducks will sometimes take up residence in backyard ponds.

BUILDING A PURPLE MARTIN HOUSE

Purple martins love to eat mosquitoes, and as such have endeared themselves to generations of gardeners. Unfortunately, house sparrows and starlings have pirated away purple martin homes for generations as well, ever since being introduced.

But a set of gourd homes can discourage the pesky invaders and bring beautiful, swooping, insect-eating purple martins to your yard.

The best gourds are around 8 inches tall, with a neck. Make a 2-inch hole in the gourd's bottom to remove the seeds. Drill some 1/8-inch drainage holes to aid in drying and act as drains in case water later seeps in; add some ventilation holes at top. Make an entrance hole 2-1/2 inches in diameter on the gourd's side. Plug the bottom hole.

Hang gourds in the middle of a large open area, at least 40 feet from the nearest tree or house and anywhere from 12 to 20 feet off the ground. Put out your gourds when the last snow goes away, or well before you think the birds will be returning from the south if you don't get snow.

Leave the gourds up all summer—it may take the birds a while to find the new homes, and they may not take note until passing through again in the fall. Be patient.

If you do get some customers, be sure to clean out the homes at the end of each season.

It's easy to grow gourds for birdhouses. Using a trellis will help plants form well-shaped fruits.

After the fruits are thoroughly dry, drill a hole and remove the seeds. Size and placement of the entrance hole will determine which species will use the gourd for nesting.

Before hanging, make sure there are drainage holes in the bottom and a few ventilation holes at top.

Purple martins like their homes painted white and hung in large groups in the open.

MAMMALS

Mammals that show up in gardens vary from the tiny, high-powered, insect-eating shrew (which is almost never seen by people), to deer and even the enormous, lumbering moose that occasionally strays into northern yards. They run, hop, crawl, jump, climb and even fly. Different species eat everything from leaves and fruits to insects, reptiles, birds and each other.

Mammals don't migrate in great numbers like some birds, but tend to stay within a fixed range that reflects their size—the smaller the critter, the smaller the range. In their native communities, mammal populations were closely tied to food availability; in the new order, in which humans control so much, populations of some have vanished, some are adjusting and a few tend to skyrocket and cause all kinds of problems.

Unlike birds, which are active during the day, many mammals are nocturnal. This lends them an air of mystery, and often leads to confusion about the culprit when there is a problem.

With some exceptions, one being the squirrel family, most mammals do their foraging early in the morning, at dusk, or during the night and some spend most of their lives invisible underground. While some mammals have perfectly good eyesight, many rely more on their sense of smell to find food and avoid dangers. Hearing is highly developed among most mammals, too. This allows them to avoid contact with humans and hear other potential predators.

The squirrel family is good place to start, since members of this family inhabit most of the country and many have made themselves entirely at home with people. In suburban and even urban areas, tree squirrels take advantage of shade and nut trees, often reaching high densities. In the east are the gray, red and fox squirrels, in the west the Pacific grey and Townsend's squirrel. Squirrels are relatively tame and endlessly inventive about getting into bird feeders—a terrific source of food they thoroughly appreciate.

Their smaller relative the chipmunk occupies a slightly different niche—nearer the ground, caching seeds and nuts. An unusual member of the family is the flying squirrel, seldom seen because it is active only at night. This tiny mammal

A rabbit or other small mammal would feel safe from flying raptors here.

has an extra flap of skin between its front and rear legs, helping it glide long distances after leaping from a tall tree.

In drier regions squirrels take to the ground. Sonoran desert regions support several species of ground squirrels; the California ground squirrel can be a problem in crop fields. In the Midwest, the thirteen-lined ground squirrel, which eats weed seeds and harmful insects, has adapted to land being cleared for agriculture and makes itself at home on golf courses. Woodchucks—large vegetarian, burrowing creatures—have been known to drive gardeners to distraction when found munching regularly in gardens.

The tree squirrels are best known as nut and seed eaters, but they also consume fruits, mushrooms and some insects and bird eggs. The red squirrels will also eat small birds. Ground squirrel diets include grains, vegetables, seeds, acorns, mushrooms, fruits, berries, birds, eggs

Squirrels that bury hundreds of nuts each year are an important link in forest succession.

California ground squirrels eat seeds, fruits, eggs and even small birds.

and insects. Woodchucks are vegetarians, which accounts for their competition with people.

Squirrels belong to a group of mammals known as the rodents, or gnawing animals.

Unfortunately, the word rodent usually brings to mind the Norway rat and the house mouse, two pest species that were brought to North America by European immigrants. These two are truly pests that have specialized in living with humans and besides scavenging just about anything to eat, they carry diseases and tend to be associated with unclean living conditions. While these members of the rodent group are truly pests, it's too bad this attitude is carried to the many native rodents.

A few of these natives, like the pocket gophers out west, do cause problems in gardens, but many others are interesting and harmless animals. Among them are the little kangaroo mice of the desert that come out at night to look for seeds, leaping great distances and able to change course in mid-flight.

Moles live underground, frequenting tunnels made by other animals. In winter they run around under snow cover in the north, leaving complex trail patterns when the snow melts, a sign that life goes on even during the coldest, darkest months.

Vegetarians, voles are often the pests who eat bulbs and other garden plants, and they have an unfortunate habit of gnawing the bark of fruit trees beneath snow line.

Moles and shrews belong to a different group than the rodents. Both are insect eaters, but moles are designed for life underground. They have broad feet turned out—perfect digging tools. Their eyes are tiny and sometimes covered with a flap of skin. They rarely come above ground, spending their time in their extensive tunnel networks. Shrews, by contrast, are excitable little balls of energy. Always on the move above or below ground, they live brief but intense lives, moving quickly and eating mostly insects but also capturing larger prey. They taste horrible to other animals, which is why the bodies of dead shrews stay around untouched for some time.

Rabbits and hares are also common through most of our country, with species adapted to habitats ranging from northwoods to the desert southwest, and from the swamps of the southeast to the agricultural areas of the midwest.

Rabbits and hares are strictly vegetarians who browse on green, leafy growth in summer, and twigs, buds and bark in winter. They spend most of their days hiding in sheltered places, emerging in the early morning or evening to forage.

Rabbits often nest in shallow depressions.

Red squirrels prefer coniferous forests.

Eastern chipmunk.

Some gardeners consider rabbits and hares major pests. Population pressures and the amount of other food available must play a part, as does the availability of young, tender plants.

Carnivores most likely to come to the wildlife garden include weasels and skunks, raccoons, ringtails and foxes. These meat eaters consume a mixed diet of insects, small rodents and plant foods and are important for controlling populations of smaller animals. Rodents, especially, have an incredibly high rate of reproduction and can become troublesome if allowed to go unchecked.

Like other mammals, raccoons, skunks, weasels and even foxes are getting thoroughly used to living with people and have discovered pet foods, too.

Everyone has raccoon stories; raccoons delight in figuring out complicated ways to foil people, and have learned to open doors and refrigerators to find easy food. They'll eat just about anything (especially corn).

Skunks (striped, spotted, hooded or hognosed, depending on your region) can afford to be bold, since merely a sighting of them is enough to scare off any human. One gardener described her whole family peering helplessly into their house from the window, as a mother skunk (who had led her babies through the dog door) finished off the dog food under the kitchen table. But skunks are not bad to have around. They don't eat plants. Their usual diet

Water is the most reliable way to attract animals.

Skunks are bold even in broad daylight.

includes mice, beetle grubs and other small creatures. If skunks are digging in the lawn, there are sure to be grubs out there.

Ringtails, similar to raccoons but more slender and with longer tails, are good mousers in the southwestern states. They also eat insects, small mammals, birds, fruits and lizards and are generally considered beneficial to have around.

Weasels, which normally eat rats, mice, ground squirrels and other rodents, will also come to bird feeders for suet and kitchen scraps.

Foxes are getting to be more and more common around people. They've had to adapt. Wherever there are denning sites (such as thickets, wooded areas or abandoned fields) and a source of food (which means populations of rodents or rabbits), foxes are a possibility. In many areas, red foxes are becoming a regular sight. Even the forest-dwelling grey fox is

Members of the rabbit family inhabit most of North America's ecoregions.

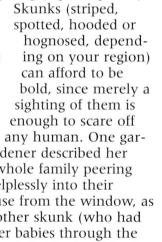

Raccoons will eat just about anything they can find.

Unfortunately, ornamental plantings are a favored browse for deer.

adapting to suburban life in some areas.

Among the hoofed mammals, only the deer is a regular garden visitor. Reactions to deer span the gamut, from Bambi lovers to those that consider deer, in the words of one writer, "house rats with hooves." While some gardeners are thrilled to see deer, and will even feed them, others hate them bitterly for consuming favorite ornamental plants and edibles.

What has happened to deer populations is a good example of how people affect other species, directly and indirectly. Deer populations have gone up and down over the years as people cleared forests or let them grow back. Since their natural predators have been virtually eliminated, and more and more land is being converted from forest to luscious ornamental plantings and edge habitat that is perfect for deer, herds are enormous and hungry. Dealing with deer is a challenge (see chapter 8 for some suggestions).

In the desert southwest, one other hoofed animal sometimes makes an appearance—the wild peccary, also known as the javelina. The pig-like native animals roam in herds of up to a few dozen. Some gardeners encourage them by leaving out food scraps on low platforms and are rewarded by early morning or late afternoon glimpses of the geay and black-haired animals. They eat nuts, mesquite beans, berries, fruits, cacti, grubs and bird eggs.

Two other interesting animals are the opossum, North America's only marsupial, and the armadillo.

Opossums live in the eastern states and have been introduced to California. They are mostly carnivorous, but will eat just about anything and will even forage in garbage like raccoons.

Armadillos, the odd, armor-plated natives of Mexico and Texas, are relatives of the sloth, something difficult to believe when you see them scurrying for cover in the forest. Although gardeners often complain about the digging these creatures do in gardens, they are largely beneficial. At least three-fourths of their diet is based on insects,

The red fox is adapting to life with people.

Javelina, wild peccary of the desert southwest.

primarily beetles, but also spiders, centipedes and other ground dwellers.

The most misunderstood group of all among the mammals are the bats. These flying animals are among the most beneficial to have around gardens, yet they are feared and often attacked by otherwise rational humans. Their mosquito consumption alone should endear them to people. As they lose their natural roosting sites in forests and caves, numbers are dwindling (see sidebar).

Water

Like birds, mammals need water to survive. A few desert

Opossums are the only marsupial in North America.

mammals can manage to obtain all the water they need from plants, but most mammals need to drink regularly.

Shelter

In a forest, what looks like a mere stand of trees with a lot of stuff lying on the ground is actually a whole neighborhood with apartment buildings, single family dwellings and major complexes, all connected by trails marked with scents and scats and other indications of who lives there.

A snug hole in the tree, started by woodpeckers and enlarged by other tree nesters, may be a warm home for a family of squirrels, or a place to stash hundreds of seeds and nuts. Fallen limbs piled on each other become a brushpile haven for rabbits, weasels or foxes. The hole in the base of a dead tree is where raccoons might spend the winter, while the tunnels under ground are alive with all kinds of creatures that share the space or take turns raising families.

High on the list of shelter sites are thickets, hedgerows, brush piles, rock piles and

caves. Mammals use them to escape predators, raise a family or spend the day sleeping. In hot climates, shelter from the sun is crucial and shady spots beneath trees and shrubs are important. Places created by people often provide great shelter; attics, basements, under porches, abandoned barns, rock walls, foundations and culverts all make great escape places.

Interaction with Humans

The rule about not touching animals is especially important with mammals since they can readily carry diseases that affect humans. Skunks are notorious for carrying rabies, for instance. Rabbits may carry tularemia. White-tailed deer may be infected with deer ticks and lyme disease. These are things to keep in mind, especially when explaining to children about wildlife around the home. If a mammal lets you get close enough to touch it, something is wrong; back off and let nature take its course or call the local branch of your state's wildlife department.

Armor-plated armadillos dig relentlessly for grubs.

Bats, the Good Guys
Advice from Batman

Merlin Tuttle, also known as Batman, has worked with bats for 25 years. He says he's never come across an aggressive bat, and finds that people often blame bats for things they never did.

The night-flying mammals are much more closely related to primates than rodents, and in the tropics and subtropics are important pollinators of many fruits, including avocados, dates, figs, peaches and mangoes. In North America, some bats are pollinators, and others a crucial part of bug control. One mouse-eared bat can eat 600 mosquitoes per hour; imagine what a whole colony accomplishes each night!

Bats can see and hear like other mammals, but they also communicate like dolphins, with sound, which makes them able to find food in total darkness. It also makes them excellent navigators. Their swooping flight pattern is disconcerting to people, but they have no intention of becoming tangled in anyone's hair. Bats that stray into living areas of houses are usually young ones that are disoriented and scared—they just want to get out (and are unlikely to repeat the mistake).

Bats do not have rabies any more than other animals, and since they seldom come in contact with people, the chances of spreading disease are minimal. Few bats have teeth strong enough to break human skin and would bite only in self defense. The so-called vampire bats are limited to a few species in Latin America that feed on cattle—not people.

Bat food is primarily insects, though a few eat fish, mice or fruits and nectar. Bats' presence is an indicator of a healthy environment. Besides mosquitoes (of which they eat many), they like corn borers, grain and cutworm moths, potato beetles and grasshoppers. During the day bats roost in a dark place, often in large groups. During cold

Bats eat thousands of mosquitoes in a single night.

winters, they hibernate.

Some of the more common bat species include the mouse-eared and the little brown bat, most common in the northern two-thirds of the U.S. and into Canada. These are small bats, and they often hunt mosquitoes near water. They like to roost where the temperature is high and stable—hence, their attraction to attics.

Big brown bats are larger, often forming colonies in buidings behind chimneys, in wall spaces and under eaves. These bats are hardy, often staying active in November and even December. They often hunt over meadows or city streets, and even around city street lights. Beetles are a favorite food.

The small evening bat of the

southeastern U.S. gathers in colonies behind loose bark, in Spanish moss, in hollow trees and beneath dead palm fronds.

In the western U.S., the pallid bat—yellowish to cream colored with big ears—is common from the southwest up through Oregon, Washington and western Canada. Most common in arid areas, this bat makes its home deep in the crevices of rockfaces, buildings and bridges. It feeds on the ground—crickets, grasshoppers, beetles and scorpions make up its diet.

Bats are not threatening to people, and in fact are beneficial in many ways. Though you may not welcome them to your garden, maybe you can learn to accept them.

AMPHIBIANS AND REPTILES

Amphibians and reptiles don't get a lot of positive attention from people because they are so different from us. Being called "cold-blooded," which sounds sinister, doesn't help matters. In fact, amphibians and reptiles just don't have an internal way of regulating their temperature, depending instead on the air or water temperature outside their bodies. Much of what appears to us as strange behavior is actually designed to keep them from getting too hot or too cold. Snakes and lizards also have an unfortunate habit of flicking out their tongues. It looks threatening, but they're only "tasting" the air, bringing back samples to be analyzed by special receptors inside their mouths that function kind of like a nose. Considering their important role in ecosystems, and their ancient lineage, all amphibians and reptiles deserve a better reputation, especially among gardeners.

AMPHIBIANS

Amphibians—the frogs, toads, peepers and salamanders that crawl and hop out of ponds each spring—all share the double life of being both water and land dwellers. Amphibians are an ancient group of animals, believed to be the ancestors of reptiles, birds and mammals. In the course of their lives, they transform from gill-breathing swimmer to air-breathing land animal. Because they absorb water through their skins, they are highly vulnerable to any dissolved poisons and so are extra sensitive to pollution.

Most amphibians don't travel very far in their lifetimes. For one thing, they have to return to water to breed. Yet in spite of this reliance on water, there are species adapted to even the western deserts. There, instead of breeding in spring, they respond to rain whenever it comes, quickly emerging to lay eggs while water is available. During extreme cold or dry times, they bury themselves deeply in the ground and can survive for months, even years.

Amphibians are shy, unaggressive creatures. Because they're so popular as food for birds, mammals and reptiles, they have developed various strategies for avoiding predators. One is hiding, of course. Another is protective coloring. Many toads and frogs have skin in shades of brown and green with irregular blotches designed to blend in with leaf litter, bark, sand or foliage. When they're sitting still, they are often almost impossible to spot.

To conserve moisture, some amphibians secrete a slimy covering for their skin. These coverings, contrary to popular belief, do not cause warts. But because they can be irritating to human eyes or other membranes, it is a good idea to wash your hands after handling any toad, frog or other amphibian.

Telling the difference between frogs and toads is not always easy. In general, frogs tend to have longer legs, be nearer bodies of water, sport a slender waist and have smoother, moist skin. Both toads and frogs come in many shapes and sizes. The largest frog is the bullfrog, which can be up to 8 inches long and leap up to 3 feet. Although originally an eastern species, it has been introduced to the Pacific coast.

Other common frogs are the leopard frog of streams and ponds, forest wetlands and meadows; the wood frogs; and the Pacific tree frogs, which have special sticky discs on their feet to help them climb.

Small amphibians don't need much space to make a home.

Red-spotted newt.

Shelter

Amphibians rely on plants for cover. Leaf litter, low-growing ground covers, vines, grasses, even even large flowers can be good cover for amphibians. Frogs sit quietly among the plants that edge ponds then leap into the water at the slightest disturbance. Toads are likely to spend the days hidden in damp hollows in the ground, under rocks or fallen trees, beneath steps—wherever it is cool and damp.

Spadefoot toads, a distinctive group, have a sort of fingernail on their back legs that helps them dig burrows when the weather is dry. They live in sandier, drier areas. Narrow-mouth toads also burrow and share their homes with lizards, moles or tarantulas. These toads hunt for ants at night. Providing good shelter is often the main way to attract garden allies such as these.

Reproduction

When it is time to lay eggs, amphibians head back to water.

Bullfrogs are known for their deep voices and huge size.

The animals have a homing instinct to return to their hatching grounds when it comes time to mate. That's why there are sometimes mass migrations of frogs across roads that have been built on traditional travel routes. It is also why a garden pond, once it has attracted a toad or frog that has laid eggs there, may well see plenty of them returning the following year. Some salamanders also migrate en masse. In California, some residential streets are closed to traffic when newts are migrating to breeding sites, a fine example of humans being willing to adjust to other species' needs.

Toads come in many varieties and sizes too. Likely in gardens are the western, Woodhouse's and American toads. The only pesky toad is the giant toad of Florida that has been known to devour large quantities of pet food, and scare off dogs with its ability to squirt toxins at targets 3 feet away.

Salamanders vary tremendously in size, shape and habits. The huge hellbenders are more than 2 feet long, live in water and eat fish, frogs, crayfish, water insects and snails. Spotted salamanders—dark blue-black with bright yellow spots—spend most of their time eating insects underground. The Pacific and Appalachian regions have many species. Many are so small and secretive they are rarely seen.

Food

Amphibians are important consumers of insects and other invertebrates. The larger ones may eat small mammals and even birds, but most focus their attention on insects and larvae, spiders, crustaceans, worms, slugs and snails. Amphibians are most active at night, taking over as pest patrol in gardens when birds are sleeping.

A healthy green frog; frogs are a good barometer of water quality and general health of the ecosystem.

REPTILES

Anole in green phase.

Reptiles—lizards, snakes and turtles—have tough skins, often dry and scaly. Turtles of course have shells. These coverings protect reptiles from water loss, and allow them to be active during the day. But because of protective coloration and their tendency to sit very still, reptiles are often hard to spot.

The highest concentration of reptiles is in in the south and southwest. Some members of this group are endangered in the wild too; some species of turtles have been collected as pets so much that many are becoming scarce. Snakes are so feared that people often kill them for no good reason, even though the vast majority of species are perfectly harmless to humans and in fact provide valuable services such as pest control.

Lizards

Lizards have a shape similar to that of salamanders, but are easy tell apart: lizards have scales, claws, dry skin and move very fast. Having lizards around is like employing a team of highly efficient pest patrol agents.

The southern alligator lizard, native to grassland and woodland edges, eats black widow spiders, scorpions, insects and other small invertebrates. Whiptails and racerunners are so used to being in motion that when they are not flitting about, they walk in place. Their favorite foods are grasshoppers and beetles. In the midwest and west, fence lizards, a kind of iguana, sun themselves on fences. Tiny anoles are friendly creatures familiar to gardeners in the south. Anoles are brilliant green when on leafy vegetation, but can change to brown as they

cool down and move to the bark of trees. The only lizard known to eat garden vegetables is the chuckwalla, which likes to munch on leaves, buds, flowers and fruits.

There is something fierce looking about the horned lizards of the desert southwest. Perhaps we've been exposed to too many movies in which huge lizards are made to be scary predators. But the only lizard to avoid contact with is the Gila monster of the Southwest. When it bites, it injects a neurotoxin into its prey that works on mammals and birds, but not frogs. It is seldom fatal to humans. All the other lizards are harmless, and are important allies in controlling insect populations.

When weather is cool, lizards will bask in the sun to bring up their body temperatures. When it gets too hot, they need shade. Birds, larger reptiles and mammals prey on lizards, searching such lizard hiding places as rock walls, crevices, under low-hanging shrubs and under leaves of plants.

Snakes

It's too bad so many people forget their childhood fascination with snakes and lizards. In some parts of the world, snakes are valued as mousers and are even sacred animals.

The problem, of course, is those few poisonous species, which have given the rest a bad name. The vast majority of snakes are totally harmless, and important in keeping rodent populations under control. Moving without legs and able to open their mouths so wide they can swallow prey bulkier than they are, snakes can pursue small rodents right into their burrows, or survive weeks without food.

Northwestern garter snake, one of the many beneficial garden reptiles.

Different species are adapted to everything from life in water to desert, and from the ground to the trees. When they come in contact with humans, their main goal is to get away.

Milk snakes eat rats and mice.

In fact, there are only four poisonous species in North America. Three of them are called the pit vipers: The rattlesnake, the water moccasin or cottonmouth and the copperhead. The fourth is the coral snake. The most effective way to prevent problems if they do happen to show up in a garden is to leave them alone (see chapter 8 for additional suggestions). Learn to identify the poisonous snakes in your area; welcome the rest.

Long-time gardeners often have snakes that have lived with them for years. Most often these are garter snakes, a group of about two dozen species that grow 2-4 feet long. They're good swimmers and eat small fish, frogs, earthworms, snails, slugs, insects, tadpoles, salamanders and small mammals. They can live up to 10 years, and often occupy the same spot year-in and year-out.

One gardener showed me a tiny hole in her house foundation that has been home to a small garter snake for years. She wasn't sure if it was the same one or perhaps a dynasty. On nice days it suns itself on the porch.

King snakes are also common throughout North America. Striped like a zebra (a dark black or brown with yellow) and 3-5 feet long, they eat other snakes including the poisonous pit vipers.

Milk snakes (see photo) love to eat rats and mice. Another good rodent controller east of the Mississippi is the rat snake. It lives in trees, under brush and mulch piles and inside old buildings and can become rather tame. It comes in different colors, usually yellow or orangish; a red version is sometimes mistaken as a copperhead, so it's worth becoming familiar with it.

Some snakes mimic poisonous snakes, which may help them in the wild, but when it comes to humans this means unnecessary deaths. One of the most useful snakes, the gopher snake, is among them. This snake of the western United States likes cultivated land and brushy desert habitat where there are plenty of rodents. It feeds on rats, mice and gophers, along with ground squirrels and birds.

Unfortunately, it mimics the rattlesnake, though it has no rattles, and so is often killed. The hognose snake, which has an odd turned-up nose it uses for digging out toads, will make a hood like a cobra when threatened.

Snakes are natural controls for many rodents that have amazingly high rates of reproduction. Without snakes, populations of gophers, mice, rats and others can soon get out of control. It may be difficult for anyone conditioned for years to fear snakes to entirely change that attitude to affection, but that isn't necessary. Just leaving them alone is sufficient.

TOADS, GARDENER'S BEST FRIEND

In 1904, an A.H. Kirkland wrote Farmer's Bulletin No. 196, entitled "Usefulness of the American Toad." He included these bits of ancient folklore (which he later refuted in defense of the toad).

If you kill toad, cows will have bloody milk.

If you handle toad, you will have warts.

But he also referenced some ancient folklore wisdom indicating that toad-watchers in times of old also had some idea of the toad's redeeming qualities.

If toad appears in cellar of new house, brings good fortune.

Toads truly are a gardener's best friend. They seldom overwhelm you with sheer numbers, because many species don't even lay eggs until they're four years old. They are homebodies, often living in the same area for years and years, providing you with environmentally-friendly, free pest control. And they eat creatures

you don't necessarily want around.

Toads emerge at dusk from their hiding places in damp, dark spots. They patrol roadsides, gardens, lawns, sidewalks and their edges, mown fields...wherever there are lots of insects and no tall grass or other plants to block their progress. Filling their stomachs four times every 24 hours, toads pack themselves with the likes of insects of all types, moths, crickets, cockroaches, grasshoppers, ants, beetles, sowbugs and weevils.

A toad will often sit perfectly still until a fly, mosquito or moth appears. When ready, the toad will flick out his tongue to subdue the flying insect, often catching it in flight. A sticky coating covers a toad's tongue, holding the prey long enough for the toad to swallow it whole. Slower prey that toads relish include cutworms, canker worms, tomato worms and cabbage worms; toads devour these caterpillars at an opportune time—when they're on the ground searching for places to make their cocoons.

In fact, back in the early 1900s

when Kirkland's study was conducted, English gardeners were known to pay for toads to stock into their gardens! So we as gardeners should add another tidbit of wisdom to the collection of toad folklore:

If you have a toad in your garden, he is your ally and friend.

Toads were once sold to gardeners as pest controls.

Small turtles like to bask on logs in ponds.

Turtles and Tortoises

The word turtle often refers to any of the shelled reptiles, although there are distinct groups, including marine turtles, fresh water turtles and land tortoises. Only the last two groups show up in gardens.

Most freshwater turtles live near ponds or lakes, and are particular about their habitat. But even a small pool can be a satisfactory home, as long as the turtle is free to come and go. There are four main groups: the bottom walkers, basking turtles, softshells and box turtles.

Among the bottom walkers are the snapping turtles that can reach enormous sizes—up to 250 pounds. They have powerful jaws that can inflict damage on unwary swimmers who step on them.

Baskers are among the most common in garden pools, named for their habit of lying around on logs or rocks at the pond edge, sometimes piled on top of each other. They disappear quickly into the water when startled.

Box turtles, the kind most likely to wander into gardens, have high domed shells into which they can completely withdraw, shutting up the openings with a hinged flap. They are common in eastern forests and fields and even venture into urban areas. They eat a variety of foods: slugs, snails, centipedes and caterpillars but will on occasion nibble on tomatoes, apples, watermelons, mulberries or strawberries.

North America has four species of tortoises, land dwellers adapted to dry areas. One species, the gopher tortoise, lives east of the Mississippi, inhabiting the coastal plain of the southeastern states, where it makes huge burrows underground among the long-leaf pine and scrub oak sandhills, and in old pastures. Some gardeners in the area have reported them as residents in their yards for 25 years.

It's tempting to think about bringing a turtle or two to live in the yard. Unfortunately that kind of thinking has led to major population declines in some species. Hikers in woodlands who decide to abduct a turtle may be breaking laws. Steve Parren, a wildlife specialist for the state of Vermont, feels strongly on the subject. If turtles wander into your garden, he says, enjoy their presence. But do not confine them, and never collect them in the wild, no matter where you live. The only exception to this would be rescuing one from danger, and even then, releasing it back to the wild is the best course.

Eastern box turtle.

INSECTS AND OTHER INVERTEBRATES

We now come to the most misunderstood and underappreciated group of living things—invertebrates. Scientists divide the animal kingdom into two main groups: vertebrates (animals with backbones) and invertebrates (animals without backbones). More than 90% of all animal species on earth fall within the latter group.

Insects make up the largest class of invertebrates. In fact, there are more insects in the world than any other living thing! It can be humbling to realize that insects and other invertebrates like slugs and snails, drive most of the life cycles around us. They feed the birds we so appreciate, pollinate flowers and help turn discarded plant material into food for another generation of new plants.

Beetles

Insects are categorized into nearly 30 different groups called "orders" and of these, the order *Coleoptera*, which includes beetles, is the largest. Insects in this group have a second set of wings that is covered by a sheath. At least a third of them are herbivores, evidenced by their chewing, boring and mining of leaves. Many gardeners have had first-hand experience with pests from

Swallowtail butterfly.

Skipper feeding on a viola.

this group such as the Colorado potato beetle, the Mexican bean beetle, squash beetles and cucumber beetles, to name a few.

But other species can be beneficial, such as the ladybird beetle, which eats other plant-damaging insects, or the dung beetle, which will break down dung

Acraea moth caterpillar on pickerelweed.

Black swallowtail caterpillar among parsley.

and other decaying matter.

Butterflies and Moths

Heading the list of popular insects to attract to the garden are butterflies and moths, which belong to the order *Lepidoptera.* In their adult phase they are strikingly beautiful, and because this stage is so fleeting, they're especially exciting to spot in the garden. They also give an excuse for creating colorful, scented gardens since sweet scents lure butterflies and moths, as do masses of bright color (see chapter 6.) In fact, moths can be just as beautiful as butterflies, but these night-flying creatures tend to be less popular.

Moths also do important work in the garden, as pollinators and as a food source for birds and other creatures. The

less attractive aspect of having moths and butterflies in the garden is that in their larval stage they are voracious leaf eaters. Some, like the infamous tomato hornworm, eat remarkable quantities of plant leaves, so gardeners who are serious about having butterflies and moths as consistent inhabitants must be prepared to supply them with food. These foods include milkweeds, nettles, members of the carrot family and many other weeds, ornamental flowers and trees and shrubs.

After they finish chomping, they spend some time in a pupa or chrysalis undergoing the transformation to adult. Some do this during the growing season, others spend the winter or dry season waiting— attached to twigs, hidden under leaves or hanging below branches in a brush pile.

When butterflies and moths emerge, the adults either eat nothing or use their long tongues to sip nectar from cer-

Monarch butterflies massing before migrating south.

tain flowers. Some species have specialized needs—the monarch relies on milkweeds, for example, while others are generalists. As they move around they carry pollen, and after a sometimes spectacular mating flight the females deposit eggs on their favored host plants. The fragile

The great transformation: black swallowtail butterfly emits liquid before pupating…

…then gradually forms a protective covering within which it will finish its metamorphosis to adult butterfly.

Spring azure butterfly.

Spotted tiger moth.

friend or foe in the garden, depending upon your perspective.

adults of a few species migrate; best known are the monarchs, which mass in huge numbers and fly south to overwinter in Mexico and California.

True Bugs

Though we use the term "bug" for all kinds of insects, scientists identify only one group, the order *Hemiptera*, with this name. Some familiar true bugs are the ambush bug that lurks in goldenrod blossoms and attacks mites, scales, thrips and wasps, or the chinch and squash bugs which have been known to destroy crops. Like many other insects, true bugs can be a

Aphids

These small, sucking insects belong to the order *Homoptera*, which also includes cicadas and locusts. They have sharp mouth parts that are used to pierce plant leaves so they can extract liquid from them. To get the nutrients they need, aphids have to extract more liquid than they can absorb, which explains the honeydew that often drips from infested plants. Some ants harvest this honeydew, and guard their aphid herd carefully, stroking them to get as much honeydew out as possible. While it would seem better for the garden to be without aphids, they seldom destroy whole crops and they are an

Ladybug with its favorite food: aphids.

essential food source for beneficial ladybugs.

Bees and Wasps

These insects are part of a varied group known as the order *Hymenoptera*, which includes both social and solitary species. Most of them do not chew on leaves, but instead eat other insects, nectar or pollen. Bees are best known for their role as pollinators and they are so good at it that

Honeybees are such efficient foragers, they have crowded out many native pollinators.

Ladybug (actually a member of the beetle family) on valerian flower.

ANIMALS AS GARDENERS

Preparing Soil

Preparing soil is generally the first task of the gardener. Yet there are many accomplished soil engineers among the animals who live in the wild. Many create complex networks of underground passages—large or small, long or short, narrow or wide, some going straight down or many yards horizontally, some near the surface and many deep in the earth. Sometimes these passages interconnect, while others are carefully blocked to keep outsiders out.

While moles and other animals—even gophers and woodchucks—are digging away, they're benefiting more than themselves. As they dig and haul and churn the soil, they bring up subsoil and mix it into the upper layers. This creates air pockets deep in the soil that provide places for water to drain when the upper layers are inundated with rain. These animals, along with the smaller scale workers like ants and earthworms, also play an important role in soil development.

Planting Seeds

Planting seeds is the next task. Here too, animals are accomplished gardeners. In fact, there are ancient evolutionary patterns of cooperation between animals and plants. Many plants produce fruits specifically designed to attract birds, mammals or insects, who eat the fruit and then deposit the seeds in places where they might grow.

Squirrels, for example, are integral to forest plantings. Every year they bury countless nuts and acorns in the ground, each in its own hole, carefully covered and tamped down; many of these sprout the fol-

lowing spring. Sticky or bristly seeds catch rides on the fur of other mammals.

Even insects are involved in planting. Violet seeds—tiny, smooth objects—have a small bit of oily food attached to them which ants eat. The ants carry the seed back to their hills,

Consider animals of all kinds your garden assistants.

remove the edible treat and either discard the seed in the soil outside their home or bury it in a shallow spot ideal for germination.

Controlling Pests

As many gardeners will tell you, a garden in bloom is often a garden in peril, a temptation to countless pests who are eager to consume its bounty. Luckily, there are also many species in nature who gladly serve as pest patrol.

Above ground, birds are the most important of these agents. At ground level and on surfaces of all

kinds, reptiles and amphibians take over. Underground, the tiny shrew and its companions are important, while larger mammals like the skunk and armadillo dig out smaller pests like grubs in the soil. Insects that feed on other insects play a major role, from the larger ones that attack anything smaller than themselves, to specialized beetles and parasitic wasps.

Pruning

Pruning and deadheading helps keep plants healthy and productive. In the wildlife garden, it's possible to let nature do some of this work for you. Deer, for instance, nibble on leaves, buds and twigs and help stimulate new growth in the process. Even tiny insects like beetles help shape trees, as shown by the flat-topped look of a white pine when a beetle bores into the terminal buds. The wildlife gardening approach makes it possible to view their "work" as beneficial rather than destructive.

Completing the Cycle

Though each growth cycle must inevitably come to an end, in the wildlife garden nothing is ever truly dead or useless. What may look to human eyes like a wasteland of plants in various states of decay can in fact be a treasure trove for a variety of animals. One could say that recycling was invented by animals. A close look at any stretch of land will reveal creatures, both big and small, hard at work gathering fallen branches or old plant matter to use as homebuilding materials.

many commercial greenhouses rely upon them for this task.

Wasps aren't usually viewed so favorably, but in fact they are one of the best beneficial insects to have in the garden. They are classified as parasitoids because they use other insects as hosts for their own eggs, and in the process kill the host insect. Each type of wasp has its own favorite target. For instance, some will attack aphids while others prefer tomato hornworms. So it's helpful to learn which kinds will help most for your particular pest problem—and then do what you can to attract them to your garden.

Bumblebee, with tongue extended, ready to land on rose.

Praying Mantis

These stealthy hunters belong to the order *Orthoptera,* and they are called predators since they will eat almost any insect (but luckily not plants) that comes along; some of the larger species even eat salamanders, frogs and birds. Their twig-like bodies and greenish-brown coloring helps conceal them from their prey.

Dragonfly

One of the oldest insects on earth, the dragonfly belongs to the order *Odonata.* Though they tend to gravitate to ponds and other water sources, dragonflies also travel several miles from their home base. Their appetite for mosquitoes, flies and other insects makes them welcome visitors to almost any garden

Spiders

There are many different species of this group and they serve important roles as predators and as food sources. Spiders eat all kinds of insects including

Grasshoppers are great leaf-chewers.

Red-legged locust.

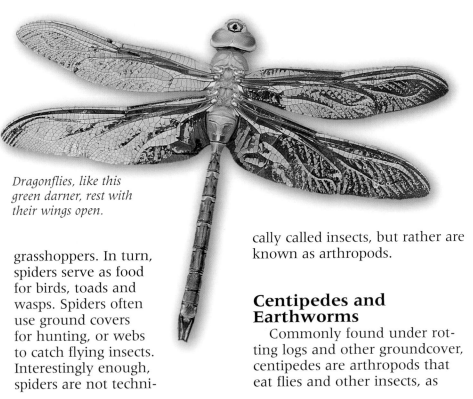

Dragonflies, like this green darner, rest with their wings open.

Fork-tailed bush katydid.

grasshoppers. In turn, spiders serve as food for birds, toads and wasps. Spiders often use ground covers for hunting, or webs to catch flying insects. Interestingly enough, spiders are not techni-cally called insects, but rather are known as arthropods.

Centipedes and Earthworms

Commonly found under rotting logs and other groundcover, centipedes are arthropods that eat flies and other insects, as well as some spiders and snails. Centipedes have at least 15 pairs of legs, and a clawlike front pincer that they use to attack their prey.

Earthworms are one of the most beneficial invertebrates to be found in the garden. Rather than just tunneling through the soil, they do in fact eat it. In doing so, they help aerate and enrich the soil substantially.

Hornet feeding on lovage.

The praying mantis will eat anything it can catch.

Spiders are an important link in the garden's ecology, catching smaller insects and in turn becoming food for birds and mammals.

◆ CHAPTER 3 ◆

STRATEGIES FOR WILDLIFE GARDENING

Gardens provide habitat for humans and wildlife; the challenge is to find those plants and patterns that please both. It takes a switch in consciousness to see the garden as animals do, as a source of food, shelter and water. Things of which gardeners are often proud, like a perfect lawn, are of little use to wildlife. To wildlife, a tangled, neglected mass of brambles or the "problem" wet area may be the real treasure.

People have widely different goals for their gardens. If less work and more time to relax are important, then wildlife gardening can be the best possible solution. As with any kind of gardening, the best approach is to start small, choosing one or more of the strategies noted here, and letting your wildlife garden evolve gradually.

In this great wildlife yard, paths wander through ferns and flower beds. This blends cultivated and wild areas, and leads wildlife into the garden.

1. KNOW WHAT'S OUT THERE NOW

Your first step to wildlife gardening is taking a new look at what is in your garden already. The National Wildlife Federation (see page 151) has a terrific form for starting this process. The two-page questionnaire about what the garden offers wildlife asks the applicant to list plants on the property that offer food, shelter and places to raise young; sources of water; and any feeders, nest boxes and other structures the gardener has added. Barbara Nardozzi, whose garden has status as an offical wildlife habitat, says filling out that form forever changed how she viewed her property.

Although an accomplished gardener when she started, she was astonished at all the plants she had never really looked at before, and about the wildlife value of others. Since then several brushpiles have been saved from burning and she now refers to two dying maples as "snags in the making."

After this initial assessment, start noting on a chart or calendar when there are blooms or fruits on existing plants. That will quickly point out where there are gaps. In an ideal garden, there would always be something to tempt animals.

Even small corners help wildlife.

2. PLAN AHEAD TO AVOID CONFLICTS

Inevitably, there will be times when wildlife and humans disagree on what plants are to be eaten by whom. Most wildlife gardeners are willing to share, up to a point. After that, good fences make good neighbors.

Steve Parren's garden, for instance, has an area fenced in for vegetables and some cutting flowers to protect them from rabbits and deer that might find those plants delicious. Plants outside the protective barrier occasionally get nibbled, and for the most part that's all right. Except one year the chipmunks went too far and challenged even Steve's patience. Such things will happen—wildlife gardening is a package deal that is not entirely under the gardener's control.

The solution is to separate the plants that are vulnerable—the ones you are not willing to share—and protect them, either singly or in a special section of the yard. Sometimes other plants can be decoys. Chapter 7 has suggestions for minimizing these types of conflicts, and discouraging animals from moving into the house with you.

Good wildlife habitat will reduce pressure on your most treasured plantings.

3. CONSIDER THE GARDEN AS HUMAN HABITAT TOO

Wildlife gardening is about sharing space, not simply turning over the yard to the wild. What do people do in their yards? It is a place to relax, to cook and eat occasionally, to play and to entertain guests. For dedicated gardeners, it is also a place to raise fruits and vegetables, and to collect and arrange ornamental plants in different ways to please them. For wildlife gardeners it is a place to observe wildlife.

Studies of peoples' landscape preferences suggest that there are many needs that come into play in gardens, and that can help in designing them for both human and wildlife comfort.

People like landscapes that have a mix of open views with clumps and corridors of sheltering plants. The idea is to have a safe place where the viewer is hidden but has a clear view of wildlife and its travel routes.

Unfortunately, in modern landscaping styles, the open view part has won out at the expense of the sheltering places. This creates fine views over vast lawns, but leaves nowhere for birds, mammals and insects to hide. Sadly, most of that space is seldom used. People need some outdoor places that feel safe, and are protected from sun, cold or other elements. But people also need views out, so they are not entirely hemmed in by tall plants, and they also need ways of moving through the landscape without being entirely exposed. There have to be chances to encounter wildlife unexpectedly.

In the Parrens' yard, lawn encircles the house, but it gets narrower each year as the flower beds expand. There is

Create places where you can enjoy the wildlife you're encouraging.

still plenty of room for running around and entertaining guests. In front, low beds allow a distant view across the field and to the hills beyond. In back, the middle of the lawn is taken up by a swing set and play area; behind one sweep of perennial garden is a gazebo almost surrounded by plantings, an inviting place to sit.

Paths wander around the island bed and off into the woods. The farther you get from the house, the wilder it is. They've also balanced the needs for views and enclosure. A second floor deck allows an expansive view, while a bench placed near a snag is a sheltered spot from which to admire flower beds.

People vary in their needs for openness and order around their homes. These needs come up quickly in any discussion of wildlife gardening. More and more, people seem to be wishing for less lawn and more wildness. Whatever the case, human beings vary and since the goal is a habitat comfortable for all, experiments and discussions are essential. Fortunately, there are many ways to accomodate human needs within an environment that also welcomes wildlife. The wildlife gardens I've visited, which tend to have more shrubs and less lawn than usual, with trees in groups, lots of flowers and an amazing diversity of plants, are generally considered comfortable and beautiful by visitors.

4. OFFER FOOD AND SHELTER

A few brush piles scattered around the garden offer shelter and nesting sites for birds, mammals and insects.

Bird feeders are often the first thing to go up in wildlife garden, and inspire next steps. While they aren't necessary to attract birds, feeders are a quick way to get started and allow a glimpse into the wildlife of a region.

But with the exception of small urban or porch gardens, the most important wildlife food sources are your plantings. Focusing on such natural sources keeps animals from relying on handouts and makes sure they get appropriate, unadulterated food. Details on what to plant are covered in chapter 5.

Shelter, too, is found largely in the plantings. A combination of evergreen and deciduous trees, shrubs, vines and groundcovers is the best approach.

And you can add structures that will make your yard even more attractive. Brush piles are among the best and easiest ways to give animals a home. Birds, small mammals, toads and butterflies will all appreciate them.

Woodpiles are another good addition. Both make up for the lack of the normal litter and piles of decaying branches found in forests. Bird nesting boxes make up for missing snags, and hollows in living trees. But there are

Dead trees, also called snags, are an important wildlife resource. Covered with flowering vines, such as clematis, they can even become a focal point in the garden.

cautions to be observed in putting them up (see chapter 6). Toad homes are a simple way to encourage these highly beneficial amphibians (see below).

Sometimes it doesn't take much!

Bird feeders are a great way to get a glimpse into the bird life in your area.

5. ADD WATER

We all have homes with running water available at the touch of a faucet, so it's easy to forget how important access to water can be in the wild. Most animals need access to water just as we do. Humans have appropriated not just land; we have often altered water patterns over large areas, drying up streams and lowering water tables. In cities and many suburbs, open water can be in short supply. Offering a reliable water source is one of the easiest ways to attract regular visitors to the yard. This is so important, we devote a whole chapter to this topic.

Small ponds like this help make up for the loss of wetlands to development.

Bird baths are most attractive to birds if near cover; bee balm, achillea and black-eyed Susans also attract butterflies.

TREES AS ECOSYSTEMS

The massive southern live oak is a whole world in itself.

Trees can totally transform the environment. For example, within the canopy of a single giant live oak in southern Louisiana is a whole world. The temperature beneath the massive, gnarly limbs is up to 20 degrees cooler on a hot, sunny day. Light levels are kept lower by the evergreen leaves, too, and the welcome shade is sought by people as well as wildlife. The furrowed trunk and branches are home to resurrection fern, Spanish moss, orchids and many other mosses and lichens. Squirrels and a wide range of birds make their homes in and around the tree. Thousands of spiders and insects live there and just about all the mammals of the region feast on its abundant sweet acorns. Such trees are an invaluable resource for wildlife, and anyone lucky enough to have one should treasure it. They are miniature versions of what goes on in a forest. A big, old white oak in the midwest serves a variety of wildlife in a similar fashion.

6. RETHINK YOUR LAWN

An informal cottage garden with its variety of plants, soft edges and smaller open areas, feels relaxed and attracts wildlife.

Anyone interested in encouraging wildlife tends to quickly reassess long-accepted notions about lawns. There is no denying that a bit of lawn is a pleasure. Visually, it satisfies a need for open space. It's a place to have picnics, to play games, to lie down or roll around with kids. A neat lawn sets off flower borders nicely, and a good lawn is pleasant to walk on barefoot.

There's nothing wrong with lawn space, but too much of it is not good for wildlife or the environment. Most lawns are too simple, too foreign, too big and too widespread. Most are made by planting a few species of European grasses adapted to a cool, mild, moist climate. In our hot North American summers these lawns must be watered, fed and fertilized so that they will stay green and keep growing long after they'd like to go to seed. They're also sprayed with herbicides to keep out unwanted "weeds" that incessantly invade this unnatural situation. Each time these chemicals are added, the life of soil organisms below is totally disrupted and any animals that feed on them may get sick or die.

Meanwhile, the large expanse of green is terrifying to small animals trying to remain invisible

Separate, neatly-edged island plantings in a large, perfect lawn can be intimidating to wildlife looking for cover.

Moist, shady garden spots give shy creatures like toads a place to live.

from predators. The area is colder, hotter, drier, windier and sunnier than the trees and shrubs it probably replaced. Amazingly enough, such artificial environments are maintained throughout the continent, even in areas where scarce water makes them entirely inappropriate.

That doesn't mean all lawns are bad or lifeless. On the contrary, less formal lawns teem with life. Native grasses adapted to specific regions—and mixed with native flowers and the weedy dandelions, daisies, buttercups and clover—attract butterflies, bees and grasshoppers, while earthworms and ants busy themselves underground. Robins, jays, mockingbirds, sparrows and goldfinches come to feast on plentiful insects and seeds.

Even without replacing the sterile European lawn grasses, it is possible to have lawns that offer advantages for people while still encouraging wildlife.

For years I lived in a rural town where the average lawn size seemed to be about two acres. My lawn was always pretty weedy, but one year, bored and tired of the whole business of mowing, I decided to go around a clump of orange hawkweed in one section, and let the wild strawberries in another section fruit before mowing that area. Eventually whole areas were allowed to grow up as I mowed only paths. And the wildlife loved it. Other gardeners, I have found, have done similar things.

In shady places, mosses often begin to take over if allowed. The Pacific northwest has some fine show gardens that feature mosses as ground covers, a perfect solution in that cool, moist area with tall trees. Barbara Nardozzi has found this principle to work in her New England garden, too. Each year the grass under some tall trees is getting thinner, and a woodland path covered with moss is a soft place to walk quietly.

Yet wildlife gardening need not spell the end of the lawn. In fact, small and simple lawn shapes and patches are one of the best ways to offset shrub plantings needed for attracting birds and other animals. It simplifies the design, and creates the edge habitat that all the animals—furred, feathered and insect alike—need.

The thing to avoid is a vast expanse of unbroken lawn. Smaller, open areas next to sheltering trees and shrubs are inviting to birds, butterflies and other animals. A good solution for gardeners in northern areas who don't like to mow is one of the new slow-growing mixtures. Talk to your local nursery for specifics. Many gardeners who have planted the mixes typically mow only once or twice a year. Because of this minimal disturbance, and no need for chemicals to maintain it, there is minimal impact on the wild creatures living there, and it certainly saves work!

Woodland paths, covered with natural materials, encourage strolling and a chance to encounter wildlife in unexpected places.

7. THINK DIVERSITY

Diversity here applies to both the plants you choose and the kinds of plant communities you build. The less lawn, the more chance there is for diversity. The ideal wildlife garden has a variety of habitats: sunny and shady, closed and open, dry and wet, tall and short, sparse and dense. By using a combination of trees, shrubs, flowers and grasses, gardeners can create a surprising range of conditions in even a small garden.

Carefully landscaped yards too often have specimen shade trees dotting the lawn, lower branches trimmed, the area below kept open and mowed. The trees are widely spaced so that each can develop an open-grown shape in full sun without competition from neighbors.

This image is so common that we take it for granted as right.

But when you think in terms of how other animals move through the environment, this picture begins to look distinctly odd. How would a rabbit, for instance, manage to get through the area without being immediately spotted by any overhead raptor? Ground nesting birds have no place to call home. Neither do birds that need vines and shrubs to feel safe. There are no layers as there are in the forest.

What's the best alternative? Small pockets that mimic natural communties. Once I was talking with a friend about possible additions to their plantings, and had come up with a list that included crabapples and a

A sunny meadow planting might include rudbeckia, asters, goldenrod, helenium, lobelia and echinacea or purple coneflower.

sycamore. Their daughter, age 11 at the time, surprised me by saying she wanted a birch grove and a meadow.

She had intuitively grasped the notion behind habitat gardening. A birch grove implies a group of trees, not a single specimen. There may be undergrowth of ferns, and seedlings of other trees and shrubs getting started in the dappled shade. This provides good cover for birds and rabbits. It is a place rich in insects, nesting

Strive for diversity in both kinds of habitat and plant species.

Animals have made a shelter within the dense foliage of cotoneaster.

Robin eggs among the raspberries are a reminder to tread softly during nesting season.

Clumps of birches will soon gather an understory of other species (often planted by birds) that together make for a rich wildlife habitat.

sites and food in the form of buds, catkins, seeds and bark.

The wildflower meadow, by contrast, is an open and sunny place of flowers and grasses that changes through the seasons as different species flower and set seed, providing nectar, food and cover for many animals both above and below ground.

In a garden, neither the grove nor the meadow need to be large expanses. They can include both native and cultivated plants. The whole scheme is a gesture, not a reproduction.

The birch grove with daffodils planted among the trees would be beautiful in spring and also feed early pollinators foraging for food. The meadow may have a tree here or there, creating more of a savanna effect.

Another possible community is a patch that mimics more mature forest. By combining taller trees with shrubs you can create a layered habitat that increases the number of potential homes for wildlife. Insects, amphibians, birds and mammals can feel safe and find food. It need not be a tangled mass. The idea is simply to think in terms of groups of plants, not single trees, and to think vertically as well as horizontally.

The whole wildlife garden should be a unit, connecting the different sections even as you make them distinctly different. Shrub borders and perennial beds are great connectors, allowing animals to find their way easily through the property and tying the plantings together visually. Masses of trees and shrubs, together with vines, make good boundaries, and can also serve as backdrops for perennial borders. Birds and almost all other creatures love edge environments…those are the havens you need to create.

Virginia creeper is a great vine for wildlife gardens, producing abundant fruits and turning a brilliant red in fall.

Leave some areas of grass uncut to allow rabbits and ground nesting birds to raise their families.

FOREST: A DYNAMIC SYSTEM

Most trees in the wild grow in groups, in company with smaller trees, shrubs and vines. Instead of one big tree, like the live oak described earlier, many different species grow close to each other.

Check out any healthy forest and you'll see it. There are young saplings and medium-aged trees, along with mature and decaying individuals of various species. Some are understory trees like dogwood that spread their branches horizontally to expose broad leaves to the filtered sunlight; others are giants like the hickory that grows tall and straight. Vines thread their way up the canopy. It's a dynamic, complicated place, with no regard for regular spacing. It isn't tidy but it's easy for wildlife to move through and find hiding places, foraging spots, places for nests and food storage.

Shrubs play an extremely important role in native communities and thus are also essential in the wildlife garden. Yet they are often neglected. With all the focus on specimen trees and trimmed hedges, the shrubs somehow get lost.

But shrubs are a crucial part of layering the garden, as understory, like azaleas in the southeast, or as an edge, to step down taller tree foliage to the ground. Among the shrubs are also many fruiting types that thrive among environments like forest edge, streambanks and roadsides. They display their fruits to birds and mammals with bright colors, and often bright fall foliage. Their flowers attract insects. Dense branching patterns are ideal nesting sites for warblers. In drier areas, shrubs are often the only available cover, their branches reaching to the ground so that ground-living mammals and reptiles can quickly dash for cover. It

is worth spending time getting to know this group of plants in more detail.

The ground level in forests is another place to find lessons for the wildlife garden. As noted above, the area is usually littered with leaves and fallen branches, and protected with low growing plants like ferns and groundcovers. There is no abrupt transition from this to the

soil below; rather, it is a zone where things are gradually broken down and incorporated by the many creatures that live there, feeding plants that are germinating and beginning to grow. At home here are also the many amphibians that love moist dark places. Allowing this kind of mini-habitat to develop increases diversity in the garden and means a lot less work for the caretaker.

In the wild, trees are seldom isolated plants—usually they are surrounded with smaller trees or shrubs and vines connect the different canopy layers.

PRAIRIES AND MEADOWS: A DELICATE BALANCE

Meadow plantings can be tailored to different regions, soil conditions and personal preferences.

At first blush, it sounds easy to create and maintain a prairie or meadow; just let a chunk of the yard go fallow and you're set. But in reality, prairies and meadows are complex ecosystems that need a fair amount of intervention on your part...both to get started and to maintain themselves.

The first thing you need to do is find plants that are native to your area, and use those as the basis for your prairie or meadow. Read up on the subject in books, talk to people in your local Audubon chapter or gardening clubs. There are many good suppliers of native seeds. While it's a nice idea to just let the ground go fallow, human activity over the last couple centuries has destroyed much of the wonderful diversity that was the prairie; the seeds just aren't blowing around in the wind anymore, nor are the tubers and roots creeping forth underground.

You don't need a huge chunk of ground to maintain a prairie patch or meadow, either. Any space you can afford will do—from an odd corner of the yard to a road-side buffer to a complete half-acre or acre section in the back of your property.

Next, realize that you're going to have to work to keep the prairie or meadow open. In many areas—the east and northeast, south and some parts of the midwest and mountain west—shrubs and trees are ever-encroaching and you're going to have to mow, or better yet burn, to maintain an open area that is friendly to prairie grasses and flowers. Fire is a good idea even if you live in the central prairie states—burn off the prairie patch or meadow every couple of springs (before green-up) to keep it lush and vibrant. True prairie plants thrive in such a situation; those are the conditions the plants evolved under.

Check local laws regarding burning before you strike a match.

When you see butterflies floating about the lovely summer colors of your meadow, birds ripping apart seed stalks in the fall and winter and baby rabbits hopping forth in spring, a meadow is definitely worth the effort.

8. Relax Neatness Standards and Let In Some Wildness

Most wildlife gardeners heave a great sigh of relief when they find out that weeds are not immoral, that perennials left with their seed heads are treasured by birds, and that not cleaning up the yards the way they clean their homes is okay. "It's so liberating," several wildlife gardeners have said to me as they gestured to their gardens. None of the gardens look neglected or uncared for. They just don't have that sterile, uninhabited look.

You need to know what your limits are on this, because wildlife thrives on messiness. The garden doesn't have to be a wild tangle. In fact, it often takes people a while to see that there are wildflowers mixed in with the perennials or that the greenery behind the flowers is a clump of nettles left for red admiral larvae to feed.

If you have space and can enjoy the unpredictability of wild-sown flowers in a section of the garden, the kind and number of insects, birds and other animals will increase quickly. But total chaos isn't absolutely necessary. Wildlife will visit even a neatnik's garden if offered some cover, food and water.

Leaving a perennial bed or meadow uncut through the winter means birds will visit to harvest the seed. If you've ever watched a goldfinch clinging to the stalks of dried flower heads in spring, when all else is drab, you know what a welcome sight that can be. One gardener said her whole opinion of dandelions had changed after she saw goldfinches harvesting their seeds.

Left on the ground among shrubs and trees, leaves help protect the soil and attract scratching birds that come to dig around for insects, worms and other treasures. The soil organisms protected underneath work hard to incorporate this new material into the soil.

Pruning is another activity to scale back. Shrubs with crew cuts produce no flowers or fruit. Those with lower limbs removed no longer offer instant cover to small animals. Trimming out all dead branches may make the trees look tidy, but it means less food and fewer nesting sites for birds and other tree dwellers.

Dead trees are among the most valued of wildlife habitats, so good at attracting birds that some people will actually "plant" dead trees in their yard. Before removing any dead or dying trees, consider the possibility of leaving them. As long as they do not pose immediate danger to houses, wires or areas where people spend a lot of time, they may well become a focal point.

Mowed paths through a wildflower planting increase the amount of edge habitat, help make it look neat, and are perfect for strolling.

Thistle seeds are a favorite food for goldfinches.

Birds love the bright fruits of beautyberry.

9. LEARN ABOUT YOUR ECOREGION, AND THINK OF THE GARDEN AS PART OF THAT LARGER UNIT

The best way to develop your own garden is to learn as much as possible about your immediate environment and what might have been there before it was developed. Books and nature centers are good places to find out what animals might show up, to identify what you've already seen and to find communities of plants to study for new ideas. This is not something you will master immediately—think of it as a fun, ongoing process that keeps getting more interesting.

Natural plant communities can provide inspiration. After we had the discussion about birch groves with Naomi, her mother, Judy, was out skiing and for the first time consciously noted that hemlocks often grow with birches, something that might work in their yard. Although species composition varies tremendously in different regions of the country, most areas have a combination of communities that are open, with annual and perennial grasses mixed with flowers, and others that are dominated by trees and shrubs. Look to them for models.

One of the benefits of looking to natural plant communities is that they can frequently propagate themselves in an area you let lie fallow. For instance, just watch some cattails pioneer a wet area in the north, or midwest.

Not only will such plantings attract local wildlife, they'll be relatively easy to maintain.

HEDGEROWS

Hedgerows combine elements of forest and meadow and show that human-directed plantings, if allowed to develop, can lead to wonderfully diverse habitats.

Hedgerows have a whole mythology, based on their hundreds of years of development in the British countryside. Started long ago with hawthornes, hedgerows filled in with blackberries, crabapples, elders and wild roses planted by birds perching there in fall. Squirrels and chipmunks brought in acorns and nuts to grow oaks, beeches and hazels. Grass and wildlfower seeds blew in, as well.

A succession of flowers bloom from earliest spring until frost; fruits ripen throughout the summer. Birds, butterflies, toads and hedgehogs live within the tangled growth, and foxes hunt rabbits there. Hedgerows furnished many useful items for people, from firewood and fruits to medicines. Some of the animals—rabbits and squirrels—were hunted and added to the dinner menu.

The difference between hedges and hedgerows is a big one. Hedges usually are all one species, planned to be uniform and often sheared to neat shapes. When plant diversity is low, so is that of the animal community. But a hedge can slowly become a hedgerow. England's hedgerows were simpler when young. Eventually, though, they became a new kind of ecosystem that stretched for miles across the English countryside, surrounding the small agricultural fields, connecting them to woodlots and forests.

Planting a hedgerow.

10. Add Native Plants to the Garden

One of the questions facing wildlife gardeners is whether to go totally native when adding new plants. There are good practical reasons for this, including the fact that the plants will be well adapted to the area and thus easy to care for. But most gardeners are not purists on this issue. They instead take a broad-minded approach, combining native and non-native species that please them and the wildlife they want to attract.

The definition of native is a bit tricky anyway. If a plant grows in North America is it native anywhere on the continent or only within its normal range of distribution?

Ecologists are beginning to think that for reforestation, seeds of plants as close as possible should be used. Time is the other issue. As of when is a plant native? Before European settlement? Queen Anne's lace is so thoroughly naturalized in North America most would suspect it is native, but it was brought here by Europeans. Native butterflies and other pollinators are so fond of it that it is often included in wildflower mixes and generally listed as an important species to include in the wildlife garden.

Native plants have an unfortunate reputation of scruffiness. But consider that most of the plants in cultivation today would not look perfect if left to their own devices in competition with others in the wild. Bring a wild, imperfect-looking native plant into the garden and give it good soil, enough light, room to grow and a little attention now and then, and it may turn into a beauty. English gardeners have long valued North American sumacs and goldenrods as ornamentals in formal gardens, and there are more candidates out there. Gardener Steve Parren has brought the humble silky dogwood to his front door and it is a mass of gorgeous blooms in spring. It takes trimming well, is hardy, requires no fussy care and brings in flocks of cedar waxwings when the bluish fruits develop in fall.

Finding out what is native in some areas can be a challenge, since so much land has been cleared, first for agriculture and later for settlements. Exotic ornamentals were often the replacements. Local nature centers, state and national parks, Audubon groups, botanical gardens and even fencerows and patches of vegetation left in out-of-the-way places can help you identify and locate native plants.

Fortunately, with the growing interest in wildlife and native gardening, more and more nurseries and mail-order catalogs are beginning to specialize in native plants of different ecoregions. To obtain a list of natives suitable for your area, check with your state extension service or university.

Queen Anne's lace, thoroughly naturalized in North America, attracts many butterflies.

11. AVOID INVASIVES

Multiflora rose is another extremely invasive plant that is crowding out native species.

exotic species against state or regional lists. Even if the plants do not seem to spread in your garden, birds can be carrying the seeds far and wide and depositing them along fencerows or in fields and forests. Louisiana fencerows are lined with the highly invasive Chinaberry trees, spread when birds gorge on the abundant white berries of ornamental plantings. The foliage turn a brilliant red in fall, which futher endears the trees to some people, but they are crowding out native species and seem to multiply each year. Non-native barberries and honeysuckles are major offenders, too.

The list included here is not an exhaustive one, just a sampling of some familiar trees, shrubs and vines that may seem innocuous. Their aggressiveness varies by region.

Invasives

Norway maple
(*Acer platanoides*)
Chinaberry tree
(*Melia azedarach*)
Chinese tallow tree (*Sapium sebiferum*)
Japanese barberry (*Berberis thunbergii*)
Cotoneaster (*Cotoneaster microphyllus, C. pannosus, C. lacteus*)
Singleseed hawthorn
(*Crataegus monogyna*)
Winged euonymus or burning bush (*Euonymus alatus*)
English holly (*Ilex aquifolium*)
Bush honeysuckles
(*Lonicera tatarica, L. maackii, L. morrowii*)
European buckthorn
(*Rhamnus cathartica*)
Multiflora rose
(*Rosa multiflora*)
Guelder rose (*Viburnum opulus* var. *opulus*)
Porcelain Berry (*Ampelopsis brevipedunculata*)
Oriental or Asiatic bittersweet
(*Celastrus orbiculatus*)

Some plants popular with wildlife are invasive species that should not be planted in gardens. Or, at least, they need to be kept under strict control. Unfortunately, some of those plants keep being included in lists for the wildlife garden.

To be sure you are not planting invasives, check any

Japanese barberry, a popular garden plant, is extremely invasive and should not be planted in the wildlife garden.

12. MINIMIZE PESTICIDES

While you may not be able to eliminate pesticide use entirely, it is best to try to stop. Pesticides will most certainly have a negative effect on all species of wildlife in the garden, as the chemicals travel through the delicate food chain. Pesticides will kill insects, which means less food for birds, amphibians, reptiles and small mammals. Although occasional, targeted use may be needed, be conservative in use, follow directions precisely and use the smallest amount possible.

Knowing how connected all the cycles are, and how checks and balances work among the different species in the garden, makes you think before grabbing a pesticide the minute some

creature is chewing on a few leaves. Killing off all the many insects living on a tree, for instance, disturbs all kinds of cycles—not just among the insects, but among those who eat them. If birds, frogs or toads are poisoned by eating chemical-filled insects, or driven away because there are no insects, your next attack of insects will be even more serious.

Working with predators of all kinds means less work for gardeners. That means making sure at least some of their food is available. An aphid-free garden may sound like a good idea, but what would keep the ladybugs around if all their food is gone? This may also mean letting snakes live in peace to help with

gopher or other rodent control. Each ecoregion, each garden, has its own balance to strive for, and its own cycles of populations that vary from year to year.

One chemical sometimes recommended to get rid of unwanted plants is glyphosphate. There are situations where it can do some good, especially to eradicate weeds and lawn grasses before planting a prairie or meadow, or for getting rid of highly invasive species like poison ivy. It breaks down quickly and does not persist in the soil. But it is a powerful substance that must also be used exactly according to directions because it will harm any actively growing plant it touches.

13. PROTECT YOUR GUESTS

Picture windows and sliding glass doors are great for looking out, but they kill countless birds who misinterpret the reflected

images. One of the best solutions is to protect the birds by placing a fine black mesh netting (it is almost invisible) inside the glass.

Other options include pasting a silhouette of a hawk or owl on the window or at least breaking up the reflections somehow, using branches in front of the window or a mobile made of pine cones or other natural objects.

The other major danger to wildlife is from pets. It is not fair to lure animals with food only to have them become easy prey for cats and dogs. Cats are especially destructive, killing millions of songbirds each year. Bells on their collars may warn the occasional wild creature, but cats can manage to move silently even with bells. Minimize hiding places for cats around feeders and birdbaths, and if at all possible, keep your felines inside. If birds are the main form of wildlife in the garden, letting cats out only at night will make a significant difference.

Cats kill thousands of songbirds each year. Bells sometimes help, but keeping pets indoors is most effective. Try only letting your cat out when birds are least active.

14. Use Stone Walls, Rock Piles, Fences and Paths

Spaces in this stone wall are potential habitat for chipmunks, lizards and other small animals.

Stone walls and fences aren't just barriers. For some creatures they're home. All that surface area—some in shade, some in sun—provides mini-habitats with temperatures that change throughout the day.

Fence lizards find just the right temperature to bask. Snakes locate favorite places to sun at different times of day. Birds also like fences for perching. One of the first things that happened when my sons put in a split rail fence around our garden was that birds used it as a lookout for potential insect food. All those little crevices in stone walls are tiny mini-caves for insects, reptiles and mammals like chipmunks and mice.

A few rockpiles here and there are equally appreciated. The many small sheltered areas under rocks will be havens for insects as they go about their activities.

Mowed through a meadow, or disappearing into the trees, paths make getting around the garden an adventure. Paths also benefit shy animals who can feel safe in hidden areas, and paths certainly make movement easier for turtles, frogs and toads. A good way to coexist with wildlife is to set apart some places to be totally undisturbed and always walk around them.

The best coverings for paths in the wildlife garden are organic materials like shredded leaves or pine needles, paving stones or bricks. Some gardeners use shredded bark, but others feel it isn't natural. It's a matter of expense, personal preference and suitability to your site. One factor to consider is if the path allows you to move through landscape quietly. Edgings of brick or stone can provide another type of micro-habitat; you can also allow a soft, natural edging of plants.

Lizards regulate their body temperatures by sunning on rocks, then moving into shade when it gets too hot.

15. CREATE PLACES TO ENJOY THE GARDEN

Once many years ago, when my older son was just 12 years old, I remember him demanding that I stop working in the garden and just sit down for awhile outside. He was absolutely right—I was so engaged in digging and hauling and weeding and mulching that I hardly ever took time to stop and enjoy the incredible beauty of it all. For anyone interested in wildlife, it's even more important to stop and look or you'll miss the chance to know your visitors.

The best strategy here is to create irresistible places to sit in the garden, then plan the plantings and feeders so that you will

The edge between forest and open area, shaded by wisteria, is a perfect place to sit quietly and listen to birds.

Get right in the middle of your garden to plan new projects.

A few hours in a small gazebo within the wildlife garden can feel like a mini-vacation.

see them easily. Outside sitting areas surrounded with flowers, hummingbird feeders and bird feeders are perfect; a bench in a secluded place among the shrubbery or next to a bird bath is wonderful, too. Consider benches, chairs, hammocks, gazebos and tree houses as essentials, not luxuries. Animals become remarkably fearless when they know they are safe. Relaxed, still gardeners pose little threat.

Eastern tiger swallowtail on dame's rocket.

Moonflowers are great for attracting moths.

The beauty of nature can be found in the most minute details.

❧ CHAPTER 4 ❧
WATER IN THE GARDEN

If there is one thing experienced wildlife gardeners yearn for, it's a pond or wetland. Why? Because water is a magnet for animals. The sights and sounds of water, and the diverse plants typical of wetlands, are irresistible attractions for birds, mammals, amphibians and insects. They come to drink, court, reproduce and feed. Gardeners with a stream or pond nearby are lucky; those without can easily add water sources that will make a difference.

Wetlands and ponds are among the richest wildlife habitats.

Natural wetlands are among our most diverse and exciting ecosystems, and among the most endangered. As suburbs and other developments spread, the borders of ponds and lakes are too often cleared and replaced with lawns. Soggy areas nearby, including marshes, swamps and bogs, are destroyed to create more land for building. Much of this is done by homeowners who think they're "improving" property they don't even use, by filling or draining wet areas.

Plants and animals evicted from their homes often disappear for good; others that relied on these areas for drinking water must look elsewhere. Suburban landscapes affect water in other ways, too.

Rainwater that is funneled off roofs into sewer systems does not get back to replenish the water tables below ground. As a result, in dry areas like California, local streams dry out.

Needed: Consistent, Reliable Water

While maintaining and protecting extensive wetlands is beyond the scope of home gardeners, we can supply consistent, reliable water sources for wildlife. The focus in providing water is on consistency, not size. Many of the wetlands destroyed are small ones, such as seasonal pools and puddles that frogs use to lay eggs or patches of wetland plants that fed pollinators

or caterpillars. While larger ponds with adjacent marshes will attract more species, like ducks and other waterfowl, even the smallest puddle of water, once discovered, will have its regular visitors.

There are a few cases where open bodies of water are neither necessary or desirable. In the desert southwest, for instance, many native animals get the water they need from succulent cactus fruits or from water-filled underground storage roots that some plants produce. An open pond can attract exotic, sometimes troublesome invasive species that compete with natives; for that reason, open water is not always a good idea.

When planning a pond, think about how animals will get in and out of the water.

SIMPLE WATER SOURCES

No Need to Get Fancy

Margaret and John Dye discovered a simple technique for providing water years ago. As Margaret described it, "One day John said, 'Let's put up something for the chickadee.' He put in a stake, got out the duct tape and attached a plastic cup." Ever since then, the cup has been right by the front walk among the flowers where the Dyes can keep an eye on it from the kitchen table. Chickadees and goldfinches use it regularly, and when the water level is low, the birds sometimes try to take a bath in it.

One day a blue jay managed to cling to the stake and bend its large body sideways to get a drink, and a chipmunk has

If cats are no threat, a shallow basin of water with perching space around it, placed near protective cover, is a simple and effective bird bath.

even learned to climb up several times a day for sips. When asked if they fill it every day with fresh water, Margaret laughed, and said "several times a day." They try to keep it filled in winter too, which means dumping out ice every day. When very cold temperatures set in, they eventually have to quit.

The sound of dripping water is irresistible to birds.

Frogs and toads can use ground level water basins.

BIRDBATHS

A birdbath is another easy way to add a water source to your garden. To understand how to make it useful for birds, imagine yourself as a small bird trying to get a drink or have a bath. You would look for a place that is safe, approachable from cover and yet with enough open area around to keep an eye out for danger. You'd also need a place nearby to perch and preen after a bath.

Choosing a Birdbath

When choosing a container for a birdbath, pick one that is no more than 3 inches deep in the center, with gradually sloping sides. All sorts of containers work—tops of garbage cans, plant saucers, ceramic bowls or even hollowed out tree stumps. The surface should be rough, not slippery. Adding a rock or two in the basin will give birds a place to perch; another option is to place

a branch so that it reaches into the water. That also gives dragonflies and butterflies a landing site.

Placing the Birdbath

Put the birdbath where you can see and get at it easily. You'll want to be able to see who's visiting, and birdbaths need to be kept filled and clean. Birds are creatures of habit, and once they become used to finding water in a place, they'll keep coming back, expecting to find it. If it dries up they will go elsewhere. The best way to keep from disappointing them is to plan ahead about how you will fill the basin, with hose or bucket, and arrange the system when the birdbath is placed.

To ensure the safety of wildlife coming to drink, bathe or soak, place the birdbath carefully in relation to surrounding plants and other structures. Many birds prefer to be at ground level, but if cats are a problem, place the bath at least 30 inches off the ground and out in the open. Placing the bath within 8 to 10 feet of a tree or shrub will allow birds to check the area for danger before alighting to drink or bathe. Baths placed on the ground in a flower bed or next to low-growing vegetation will attract a wide range of creatures including chipmunks, toads and frogs.

Check It Regularly

Checking the birdbath should be part of your everyday routine. A quick squirt from the hose now and then will help prevent the spread of disease. Occasionally, especially if algae begins to grow, the bath will need a more thorough scrub-and-rinse with a weak bleach solution (not soap). You may need to do this every week or every month, depending upon the conditions in your yard.

Raised basins keep birds safe from cats, and let you see visitors.

MOVING WATER

The sounds of water dripping or splashing are powerful lures for all sorts of wildlife. Birds can hear it from several blocks away. During migrating season, which can be a dry time in some regions, they will seek out such sources and even modify their routes to stop in, training their offspring to do the same.

Creating Moving Water

Fountains and artificial waterfalls are the high-tech way to create such an attraction in the garden, but simpler, cheaper methods also work. A hose draped over a branch above a water dish, slowly dripping water, is one solution. Another technique, which a gardener who uses it says "drives the birds crazy," is a 2^1/$_2$ gallon water container set on bricks in the birdbath, with the spout set to drip. It isn't elegant, but it does the trick.

There are many ingenious ways of creating moving water features, reflecting the interests and styles of different gardeners. Often these creations are of recycled materials, the only real cost being the pump. Pumps designed for use in ponds and pools are available through garden centers and catalogs, although boat bilge pumps will often do the trick. The main goal is to let water bubble up to run over rocks, drip down a surface or spill over a flat area to create a shallow stream of water.

Rocks, rubble, wood and shells are all potential construc-

Shade is important for ponds in southern areas, where water can otherwise get too hot.

tion material. Except for truly dry regions where this may be inappropriate due to conservation issues, they can be a fine addition to the wildlife garden.

Recirculating pumps make it relatively easy to add a small waterfall, which helps aerate the water.

WATER IN WINTER

In cold winter areas, gardeners who keep open water available when natural sources are frozen report a dramatic increase in activity around their homes. Depending on how cold it gets, there are several approaches. Some are simple, some more involved.

The Big Break-Up

A thin layer of ice over a water basin is easy to break up and discard. If thick ice develops, pour boiling water on it to melt it. If the whole thing is frozen solid, take the basin inside to thaw out and replace it with another container for the day. This works best if the basins are lightweight, perhaps plastic.

Get Serious

For very cold climates, or to cut down on daily chores, a small heater designed for bird-baths may be the best solution. Heaters in several different designs are available in stores that stock bird supplies and in catalogs. These heaters typically plug into a grounded outlet using heavy all-weather extension cords. When the temperature is above freezing, they simply shut off. Some commercially available birdbaths come with a built-in heater. Install them fairly close to outlets, and in locations where you can easily monitor and take care of them.

A heated bird bath supplying open water through the winter is one of the easiest ways to keep birds around.

PONDS

Water gardening in artificial ponds is catching on all over the country. Nursery owners report increased sales of liners, pumps and water plants and several magazines focus on water gardening. Many who start out with one pool add more over time and eventually create elaborate systems. Part of the reason for ponds' growing popularity is the availability of high-quality materials that are fairly easy to install.

Don't Get Too Fancy

Unfortunately for wildlife gardeners, much of the information and material available for water gardening is designed for growing exotic ornamentals and fish. Pre-formed pools have abrupt edges with steep sides, exactly the opposite of what

most wildlife needs. Turtles cannot negotiate such edges, and even frogs have a hard time getting out. Butterflies seldom feed on open water; they prefer edges of puddles or soggy soil or sand. Birds can't bathe in deep water. And goldfish and koi, so beautiful to humans, are a favorite of raccoons and herons, who can clean out a small pond in an amazingly short time.

Nonetheless, with a little thought and experimentation, artificial ponds can be transformed into a home or regular stopping place for many species of animals. Although man-made ponds develop their own ecology over time, they remain artificial systems that rely on human intervention. So before you put one in, be sure you are committed to doing the work

needed to maintain them, especially if you choose to add fish.

Simple Ponds

The simplest mini-ponds are made using half barrels and similar containers made of plastic. Old wooden barrels are relatively cheap and look nice in the garden. Some gardeners use them as-is, but there can be chemicals embedded in the wood that are harmful to plants and animals. To solve this problem, line the barrel either with heavy black plastic or with a ready-made form that can be purchased. Also attractive are some of the lighter plastic pools that look like granite. They would be more convenient on a porch in areas where they need to be moved in winter.

A half barrel can support a miniature water lily, along with

Small pools quickly add to wildlife diversity in the backyard.

several other submerged plants and floaters. To make these tiny ponds more useful for wildlife, place some branches so they reach into the water. Taller plants around the edge also help provide landing places. The problem, of course, is the edge. For getting a drink, perching on the rim may help, but birds cannot bathe unless there is a shallower area.

The same problem is there with the larger pre-formed, in-ground pools made of rigid molded plastic. They are long-lasting and come in a variety of shapes and sizes, complete with built-in shelves for potted plants. When installed, the edges are covered with flat stones that project over the water, creating an abrupt drop for any creature interested in getting into the water. Plants both outside and within the pond can help soften the transition, and dead branches placed to create ways of getting in and out and perching above the water will help.

Flexible Liners — Wildlife Friendly

Flexible pond liners are much easier to adapt for wildlife use, and you can still grow exotics like water lilies in them. While the instructions that come with these liners suggest making a shape much like the rigid plastic pools—with steep sides, shelves for plants and overhanging stones—you don't have to do that. You can vary the depth and slope of the base to encourage frogs to lay eggs, butterflies to search for water and birds to bathe.

One gardener I know made a pool just right for her turtles by digging a pool with very shallow, sloping sides that was easy for them to negotiate. Although she worried their toes might harm the plastic, they caused no problems. Another variation would be shallow, pebble-filled area for birds.

Installing A Pond

It takes about a day to install a pond. Liners come in rectangular shapes. Figure on paying about $65 for a small one that measures 8 feet by $6^1/2$ feet, with a thickness of 32 mil, more for larger or heavier ones. For a 5 by 8 foot finished pond that's 2 feet deep, you'll need a liner 11 feet by 14 feet. Most liners come with a guarantee of 10 to 30 years, so they are a long-term investment. Under the liner you'll need to install a protective layer of sand, carpeting or a purchased material, to prevent punctures by stones or other sharp objects. If the liner does get punctured, it can be repaired with a patch kit.

Waterfalls

Even more exciting for wildlife, and gardeners, is a small waterfall at pond's edge. Submersible pumps designed for this purpose start at about $35. To make a waterfall takes some experimenting with rocks, but it is not difficult. Clear or natural colored tubing helps create the illusion that it is natural. The rocks need to be backed by more lining material, or water will disappear. Besides providing interest for people and wildlife, such a set-up helps aerate the water, keeping it healthy for the pond's inhabitants.

Placing the Pond

In the north, ponds are best placed in full sun, while in southern and western regions, shade is essential to keep the water from overheating. Algae will also grow unchecked if there is excessive sunlight on the surface. One gardener reported he had put a pond away from trees as instructed when he lived in North Carolina. The pond got too hot and full of algae. So when he moved to Minnesota, he built a

Floating plant leaves help regulate water temperature and provide hiding places and perches for wildlife.

pond in the shade, and found that water lilies did poorly and would not bloom (they need at least six hours of sun each day).

In southern gardens, ponds should have protection from the south and west. The trade-off is that if it is under trees, you will have to remove fallen leaves. If at all possible, check with successful water gardeners in your area to see what they have done. Water depth has a tremendous influence on water temperature. At two feet below the surface, the temperature can be dramatically lower in summer and higher in winter than it is at the surface.

In a flat area, where you put the pond doesn't matter too much, but in uneven terrain, choosing a low spot will make it look more natural. Before digging, check for underground cables, utility lines, plumbing and remember that near large trees there are likely to be tough roots that may make digging difficult or impossible. Before starting, use a hose to mark out the potential pond edge and get a feel for how it will fit in.

SPOO'S BOG PONDS

A Wildlife Haven

Alfred J. Spoo has made a specialty of creating ponds for wildlife in his Pennsylvania garden, and has developed a system that frogs, birds and butterflies seem to find irresistible. His 12 ponds are home to 47 green frogs, along with who knows how many pickerel frogs, bullfrogs and even wood frogs (which belong in deep forest). Elusive spring peepers, usually impossible to catch sight of, are so common and tame in this garden that visitors have been able to walk right up and touch them.

A pair of box turtles breed there, spending the winter buried in mulch piles. He has counted seven species of dragonflies, another four of damselflies. Butterfly experts come to his garden to find rare species like the banded hairstreak, along with any number of more common species.

Spoo has been a wildlife enthusiast most of his life. He started his collection of insects when he was 13, and it now includes 22,000 specimens from all over the world. But his greatest joy in recent years has come from the sanctuary he has created for living creatures around his home in western Pennsylvania.

How It All Started

"The whole idea started ten years ago, after a swampy meadow near my home became a housing development," he wrote in a description of his garden. "I had spent thousands of hours there relaxing and studying nature. To fill my disappointment, I began to set up a similar habitat, but with many more species of plants. I now have 128 species of trees and shrubs and 648 other flowering plants in less than one acre of land."

Essential to attracting a great diversity of wildlife are the ponds. He has four deep ponds filled with water lilies, sunfish and goldfish, built in the style usually recommended for water gardens. After years of experimenting, he has also developed what he calls bog ponds, a special construction and planting design that is ideal for wildlife such as salamanders, frogs, toads, turtles, dragonflies and butterflies. They are a fine example of how pond technology can be adapted to encourage wildlife usage.

Building Advice

The first time he made a pond, Spoo used a flexible liner and gave it sloping edges. He put sod right up to the water's edge, wanting to make it look natural. He kept losing water, and even after emptying the whole pond and digging everything up, he couldn't find a leak. Finally, he realized that the sod was acting as a wick, drawing water right out of the pond. That's why he switched to putting in a solid footer of poured concrete to secure the edges.

His bog ponds have two sections, one for open water, the other a sloping wetland area filled with soil. Close to the open pond, the soil is covered with about 1 1/2 inches of water; at the outer edge it is above water line. In the bog section, he plants a mixture of cardinal flower, monkeyflower, boneset, sedges, arrowhead and water mint. The bog plants help keep the water clean. He uses no pumps to aerate these small bog ponds, but they stay clean and clear. Frogs lay eggs there regularly.

The larger ponds are deeper (up to 2 feet deep) and have pumps that help aerate them. Spoo has constructed small waterfalls with rocks. He says liners under these waterfalls are also essential, or the water will mysteriously disappear. Like many gardeners who have become hooked on pond gardening, Spoo has become intrigued with creating links between several ponds, via streams and waterfalls.

A secluded woodland pond, reached by a small path, is a good place to glimpse shy forest creatures.

HOW TO PUT IN A BOG POND

1 Choose a location for your pond—ideally the site should receive full to partial sun. Avoid sites near or directly underneath trees since falling leaves can cause problems. You can use a garden hose to outline the space needed.

2 Select a high-quality preformed pond shell—be certain to check that the material it's made of is safe for fish since some plastics emit chemicals that can be toxic to wildlife. Also, look for a shell made of UV resistant material, so it will hold up under bright sunlight.

3 Dig out the soil within the outlined area; 10 to 12 inches deep for the pond area, and 5 to 7 inches deep for the bog section. The bog area should slant upward gradually. Put a protective layer of sand, or other material, at the bottom of the hole to prevent stones from puncturing the liner. Check that the bottom surface is level before setting the shell in the hole.

4 Cover the excavated area with a rubber or PVC liner, leaving a generous border of at least 6 to 8 inches on all sides. Set the shell in the hole and fill it gradually with water as you backfill the space outside the shell with soil. This part is easiest if you have another person to help.

5 Install edging around the pond. First, dig a trench 4 inches deep and 6 inches wide, all around the pond. Fill the trench with concrete made of a standard mixture (1 part cement, 2 parts sand, 3 parts gravel). Wrap the excess liner over the top of the footer, then install flat fieldstones to cover the top edge. For this step, use a mixture of 1 part cement to 3 parts sand; put a 1-inch layer of cement below the liner, and more on top.

6 If desired, install a submersible pump in the pond, following manufacturer's instructions. Note: to operate properly, a pump will require regular cleaning and consistent maintenance.

7 Plant the bog garden section, then cover the topsoil with a layer of gravel. Hose it off, drain the pond and refill it with clean water.

8 Choose a variety of plants for your pond. Aquatic plants are divided into several groups including floaters, marginals and oxygenators; it's a good idea to include 2 or 3 bunches of oxygenating plants per square yard of surface area. If you want to add fish to the pond, be sure to check the water quality first.

9 Enjoy your bog garden and all the wildlife it draws to your yard throughout the seasons.

WATER QUALITY AND MAINTENANCE

Some gardeners are lucky enough to have a stream nearby to use to fill their ponds. This is ideal, since water from municipal systems almost inevitably contains chlorine. In general, filling the pond and letting it sit for a week or two will allow that chlorine to evaporate. Check water levels regularly and top the pond off to keep it relatively stable.

Let the Occupants Do the Work

Ponds are quickly colonized by a variety of plants and animals that develop their own equilibrium. If the water gets cloudy, or there is a bad smell, consult with your local extension service or other agency to find out the best course of action. Although there are chemicals sold to clear up such problems, they may contain substances that could harm wildlife. Draining the pool, cleaning it

out and refilling with fresh water may be your best solution.

Opinions on the need for annual cleaning vary. Alfred Spoo filters all his ponds each spring. He attaches a water filter to one of his pumps, and pumps the water into barrels placed around the pool. He scoops out whatever the pump can't handle and wipes the liner clean, then refills the pond with the filtered water and tops off with fresh water. He scoops out any fish or other animals and leaves them in barrels until the pond is refilled. Although it's a lot of work (especially when you have 12 ponds), he's never had a problem in any of his ponds. Other pond owners prefer not to disturb the pond and will drain it only if there is a problem.

Winter's Challenges

Winter in cold regions presents some additional chal-

A wildlife haven.

lenges, though ponds without fish are a little easier. Smaller ponds can freeze solid; they'll be fine in the spring. Spoo's bog ponds get no special attention. In the larger ponds, he keeps the water flowing by repositioning the tubes of the waterfall so they run directly into the pond. Even when part of the surface freezes, a six inch hole stays open so the fish have oxygen. Tender plants, of course, must be put in a safe place. Hardy water plants can go into the deepest part of the pool.

MOSQUITOES AND FISH

Everyone worries about mosquitoes hatching in artificial ponds and a standard suggestion is to throw in a few mosquito fish to eat the larvae. While it sounds reasonable, this is not always a good idea.

Say No to Mosquito Fish

Mosquito fish bear live young, and can reproduce every 28 days, which makes them highly prolific. In the some parts of the southwest, where they were introduced, they have wiped out local fish species. Many states' fish and game departments discourage people from introducing the species.

It is easy to think of a small artificial pond as a self-sustaining, isolated system. But, as fisheries experts point out, fish have a way of getting around so no wetland, and no garden, is isolated from the rest of the world. For this reason, before buying and tossing a few mosquito fish into your pond, check with state fisheries agencies. They may suggest a native species that would be better to use.

Keep the Water Moving

Keeping the water moving is another good way to reduce mosquito populations. Plus,

the good news is that if there are mosquito larvae in your pond, predators will inevitably arrive to snack on them. The water-living nymphs of dragonflies are among the most voracious enemies of mosquito larvae.

Stay still for a while near a wetland garden and you begin to see the fine details, like these circumpolar bluets resting on a leaf.

LARGER PONDS

The more your pond mimics a natural setting, the better it will be for wildlife. Notice especially the edges of this pond, with its shallow muddy areas and gradual transitions.

To make larger, unlined ponds it's best to get professional help. In most states your extension service can give advice on selecting a site and constructing ponds and how to get competent help. Often it is not a good idea to turn a wetland into a pond, since the wetland is often more diverse and important to wildlife. But some-times enlarging an existing pond or re-grading the bottom to make it more inviting to wildlife can make it vastly more productive.

Vary the habitat in and around any pond. Fish need deep pools for wintering, and other places to hide among rocks under the water's surface. An island can become a safe haven for nesting waterfowl. Shallow sections near the edge will invite frogs and toads to lay their eggs in spring. Rocks and logs give turtles and others a place to bask. And a variety of edge environments, from open and sunny to densely planted with sheltering shrubs and grasses, will attract a wide range of wildlife.

Casual plantings around a pond, mixing wild and cultivated species, make it easy for wildlife to get to the water safely. (NOTE: The attractive fuchsia flower is purple loosestrife, an extremely invasive species that has escaped into native wetlands where it crowds out other species. See chapter 3).

Sometimes backyard ponds get surprise visitors—two otters are checking this one out.

PONDSIDE PLANTS

Butterflies tend to frequent areas near streams and ponds. Some of the wild plants native to damp places (like the tall, pink-flowered Joe Pye weed) are among the best butterfly attractors.

Alfred J. Spoo knows his butterflies' preferences well. To complete the habitat for butterflies, on the east, south and west sides of his bog ponds he plants butterflyweed, asters, catnip, phlox and blanket flowers. Beyond them go zinnias, milkweed, teasel, cleome, Joe Pye weed and Mexican sunflower. Taller plants go on the north side and farther from the pond, so that they don't block sunlight. Among them are pyracantha, spicebush, bush honeysuckle, spirea and butterfly bushes. They act as a windbreak, a summer nesting site and a winter food source for many species of birds.

Pickerelweed, a native wetland species.

Marsh marigold.

To encourage the butterflies to actually live in the garden, he includes many larval plant foods, among them spicebush for the spicebush swallowtails, nettles for red admirals, and willow for red-spotted purples and mourning cloaks.

PLANTS

WATER PLANTS

cattails	*Typha* spp.	arrowhead	*Sagittaria* spp.
pondweed	*Potamogeton* spp.,	pickerel weed	*Pontederia cordata*
	especially sago pondweed,	yellow flag	*Iris pseudacorus*
	P. pectinatus	blue flag	*Iris setosa, I. versicolor*
widgeon grass	*Ruppia occidentalis*	sweet flag	*Acorus calamus*
	or R. maritima	prairie cordgrass	*Spartina pectinata*
bulrush	*Scirpus validus*	water lilies	*Nyphaea* spp.
wild celery	*Vallisneria americana*	lotus	*Newlumbo* spp.
smartweed	*Polygonum bistortoides*	marsh marigold	*Caltha* spp.
	P. coccineum, P. hydropiperoides		

At pond's edge, water-loving cattails mix with three great butterfly plants—goldenrod, jewelweed and liatris.

One way to regulate the temperature of any sized pond and keep algae growth at manageable levels is to make sure plant leaves cover a high percentage of the surface. In hot, sunny areas like California, up to 70 or even 80 percent of the surface can be shaded by floating leaves of lilies and other plants. In cloudier climates, 50 to 60 percent coverage, or even less, is fine. Choose a variety of plants to include—they will not only add to the beauty of the garden and the pond's ecology but will also provide shelter for wildlife. Frogs like to sit on lily pads, or hide below them, especially when predators like snakes and herons are about.

Nurseries and garden centers offer a variety of exotic plants for ponds. Some of them are fine for wildlife as well. There are miniature varieties of cattails, for instance, that do well in barrel ponds. For planting around the edges of natural ponds, and to add some native food and cover plants in pots, consider some of those listed.

Red-winged blackbirds and other birds nest among cattails. For a small pond, there are miniature cattail varieties.

Tender water lilies, grown in submerged pots, can be overwintered indoors in northern areas.

Swamp smartweed.

◆ CHAPTER 5 ◆
THE PLANTINGS

Getting started with wildlife gardening can be as simple as putting up a birdfeeder, but it tends to escalate quickly. One Pennsylvania gardener, Debbie Fluharty of Coraopolis, says that one year she and her father put up a few bird feeders and a bird bath, initially for aesthetic reasons. Two years later, they had planted raspberry, blackberry, huckleberry, cherry trees, flowering dogwoods, lilacs and creeping wintergreens—all for birds. Their whole garden had been transformed, and they didn't even try to harvest any of the fruits.

A wildflower meadow or prairie patch is one of the best ways to increase wildlife sightings around your home.

Start Small and Plan

As with any gardening project, the best policy is to start small. Adding a few feeders, a water source or flower gardens for butterflies and hummingbirds are simple changes that will quickly attract more wildlife to any back yard. If it's fall, starting a brush or leaf pile will give a few wild creatures a home for the winter.

Paying attention to what's visiting the yard is essential to planning, and you can start at any time of year. Begin by keeping track of which animals you see regularly—at feeders, in trees and shrubs and on the ground. Note where they are and what they're doing. If your own yard has no evidence of wildlife, visit a neighbor's yard or a nearby nature center to find out what might come to the yard if the right habitat were available. A lot of ideas are scattered throughout this book —feel free to pick and choose among them. Eventually, you can rethink the whole garden and plan long term.

To make this project fun it's crucial to remember that the role of the wildlife gardener is to be a participant in a system, not the creator of an idealized image. The challenge is to learn about the processes going on and to know when to step in gracefully, working with the natural cycles in the garden.

Creating a Plant Bed

Mark off a small area, cut sod several inches deep and remove in sections.

Rake to remove roots and any other large objects and add soil amendments if needed.

Space your chosen plants according to directions.

This combination of zinnias, rudbeckia, marigolds and impatiens will attract butterflies, other pollinators and perhaps hummingbirds.

LEGAL CONSIDERATIONS

Sometimes a yard designed to attract wildlife can look unconventional enough to upset the lawn-bound. Lorrie Otto, one of the pioneers of prairie gardening in the Milwaukee area, learned about this the hard way many years ago. After attending a workshop on prairies, she decided she didn't need a lawn and began to replace it with native flowers. She even brought troops of the local Brownie scouts there to teach them about Midwestern wildflowers.

One summer day, her son came running in to report that the garden had been mowed down by city workers. Village officials had responded to a complaint from new neighbors who had built a two-story house that looked down on Ms. Otto's garden. Unaccustomed to anything but grass lawn, they thought her yard was overgrown with weeds.

Fortunately, the story had a happy ending. When they realized what they had done, the city gave Ms. Otto a cash settlement, and she went on to become famous as a proponent of native plantings. Now in her late 70s, she still conducts tours of her gardens for visitors from all over the world, and many gardeners have followed her example.

Still, many communities have ordinances regulating lawns, weeds and tree plantings, especially in front yards. Before embarking on a major overhaul of your yard, check the rules. Some regulations were originally designed to check the spread of noxious agricultural weeds. Although outdated, these laws have occasionally landed wildflower growers in legal trouble.

More and more gardeners are challenging local ordinances about front yard plantings; A meadow or prairie patch like this is not only better for wildlife than the sterile lawns beyond, but cuts down on environmental pollution.

Another alternative to lawn: Birches underplanted with ornamental grasses and perennials provide shelter and food for birds.

developed in North America and is now a major industry. People spend a fortune on mowers, turf, seeds and specialized chemicals or landscaping services that promise to make our yards like the photos in advertisements.

The Art of Compromise

There is no need for a wildlife garden to be offensive, and simple compromises will usually prevent run-ins with neighbors. For example, the front yard could be kept more conventional, with the "wilder" plantings planned for the backyard. Or you could leave mowed borders around a meadow planting or use fences to set off an unorthodox planting of natives. With a little give and take, your neighbors will probably be more willing to rethink their view of the wildlife garden.

A good example of this is a garden I used to see in Baton Rouge, Louisiana. It offers a startling departure from the properties nearby, for instead of a neatly mowed lawn, it features a profusion of wildflowers with painted bird houses among them. Joggers, walkers and people pushing baby carriages always stopped to admire the show. It was clear from the sounds of birds among the shrubs and trees that they preferred this yard to others in the neighborhood. Of course some of the neighbors had a hard time with the

Breaking Yourself Away From the Lawn

A major stumbling block for many when considering a move to wildlife gardening is the lawn. It was easy for me to give up mowing a good piece of my yard because I enjoyed the mix of wildflowers that showed up, and the changing colors and textures of the grasses through the seasons. But for many people, not mowing the lawn is as offensive as leaving trash all over, and a garden without straight rows and neat edges is slovenly. This is so taken for granted that discussions about it are far from rational.

Generations have been brought up in houses surrounded by green rectangles of mowed grasses. That's just home. But we ought to be able to see beyond this pattern, to realize how conditioned we have become to the

idea that this type of lawn is "natural." It isn't. Instead, it is simply a fashion that has

Coreopsis and rudbeckia star in this prairie planting, with a supporting cast of many other species that make for a complex, varied habitat.

Imagine how much more interesting and colorful our neighborhoods could be if meadows like this one of daisies and coreopsis replaced vast lawns.

ragged look of the area when everything went to seed later in the season, but it takes time to accept the cycles of the wildlife garden, especially in times of transition.

The rest of this chapter covers overall design approach for the wildlife garden: how to choose plants, some combinations to try, and how to guide the process of transformation.

OVERALL DESIGN

Steve Parren has a wonderful expression for his approach to gardening: he uses plants to "tie the house to the land." An aerial view of his property taken 14 years ago shows a blank rectangle cut out of a forested hillside with the house in the middle. The previous owners had mowed the whole yard, leaving the land bare of anything but grass. The result, repeated all over the country in suburban settings, was a home separated entirely from the rich life all around. Fortunately, a combination of planting and allowing nature to take its course can change this fairly quickly.

Pull Nature In

The secret is to reverse the usual way we think of landscaping. Instead of imagining a vast green lawn on which to carefully arrange a house with some shade trees and a few flower beds, imagine the reverse. A plot covered with plants—trees, shrubs, flowers, grasses, groundcovers—with some open spaces for a house, a lawn, flowers and so forth, all of them tied together by paths. This is the kind of thinking that can create ideal conditions for both humans and wildlife.

In Steve's garden, the results after 14 years are nothing short of amazing. He did not start with a master plan, carefully measured and plotted on graph paper. Instead it's a work in process, one the whole family is part of, and one that considers the activities of the wild creatures that share the yard.

Large massed plantings invite wildlife in from the neighboring woods, and give them a safe place to be close to people. Note the irregular edge that softens the transition from taller plants to lawn.

A Relaxed Plan

Wildflowers in an unmowed strip along the driveway greet visitors in summer, creating an always changing, colorful border that releases clouds of butterflies in late summer and flocks of goldfinches that feed there when seeds mature. A developing hedgerow of pines and deciduous trees screens the other side, and creates a safe passage for animals crossing the property. Flower beds have been gradually taking up more of the lawn, and now wrap all around the house and the gazebo in back. A large birdfeeder and a swingset for the children occupy what's left of the lawn. Chipmunks feel safe enough to feed at any time, and a red squirrel nests in an unused box in the tool shed. Toward the edges, things get wilder, gradually blending to the surrounding trees.

Instead of constantly extending the controlled area, the Parrens invite the wild inward, making transitions less abrupt. Paths wander off into the sumac patch and toward the stream nearby.

Instead of a lawn sprinkled with flower beds, think of your garden as a rich and varied plant community in which to create openings and paths.

The wildlife garden thrives on diversity, from mature trees to colorful annuals.

STARTING FROM SCRATCH

Anyone building a new home can increase native wildlife by leaving some of the existing vegetation on the lot. Trees, shrubs, even patches of tall grasses become refuge for local creatures, especially when a large area is being altered rapidly.

If there are big trees on the property, consider placing the house away from them. Old trees are not, as most people seem to believe, tougher than young ones; they are actually more sensitive to having their roots disturbed, and the roots extend much farther than you would expect, up to $2^1/_2$ times the diameter of the crown. Protect tree roots from compacting during construction, and monitor them carefully in the following years, watering if necessary. They will more than repay this extra care by sheltering many species of wildlife.

Know What's There

Inventory the property carefully. Treasure wet areas; they can be planted with wetland species that will greatly increase the yard's diversity. Also check out the neighborhood to see what the major plantings are; instead of using all the same species, think about planting some that are different, to add to the area's diversity. Remnants of native vegetation nearby might suggest suitable plantings.

Trees and Shrubs are Important

Get trees in fast, especially around the property boundaries. Choose a combination of deciduous and evergreen trees suitable to your area and consider planting locations carefully. A tree can be used to block winter winds, screen unpleasant views or preserve desirable views, depending on where it's situated.

Plant lots of shrubs in front of and around trees, and along boundaries. Do not isolate shrubs but keep them in groups. They will provide cover and food for many species, as well as travel routes for animals coming from surrounding areas to your yard.

Mix It Up

Think of creating several distinctly different areas within the yard—some open, some shaded and some that will be left relatively undisturbed. Flower beds are best located near the house, where you can see them and the butterflies that will visit. Choose a site that is screened by the house, a fence or trees and shrubs, so the plants and visitors will be protected even on windy days. Arrange plantings so they split up the view of the yard. Fences, baffles or trellises with annual vines can help with this until plantings mature. Leave areas near the outer edges of the yard more wild.

Since you're starting from scratch, you can plant the type and size of lawn you really want. Do some research to find out which grasses are best for your region and require the least amount of work. Determine what the goal of the lawn will be and how much room you need for sitting, recreation, cooking or playing.

Plant annual cover crops like buckwheat or annual rye in areas you're not ready to seed, to help enrich the soil until you are ready to work it. This is the time to put in a meadow or prairie planting and to lay out paths. For maintaining open areas, consider low-care native groundcovers.

Expand the area by making connections with nearby natural areas. Visualize a corridor bringing animals in from adjacent streams, a park or even a neighbor's wildlife garden.

Checking a nesting box near the edge of the garden. At right is an island bed of basswood, hemlock and apple that has filled in with species planted by birds and other animals. Within its thick foliage birds nest undisturbed.

RENOVATING AN EXISTING GARDEN

If you already have a garden, start out with an inventory of what you have and make changes slowly. Many gardens that were not landscaped for wildlife nonetheless offer plenty of resources and need only a little bit of adaptation. The gardens that owners feel are "neglected" are more likely to be attractive to animals than the more manicured ones.

Create a Natural Flow

If there are isolated tall trees standing around the lawn, try surrounding them with a few smaller ones, then adding some shrubs. Or create a grouping of shrubs and trees to link them, making it easier for wildlife to move around safely. Expand the areas beneath them with mulch; lawn clippings, leaves and shredded bark are examples of good mulch materials.

Clipped hedges can make good nesting sites and offer cover, but the same plants will be far more valuable to wildlife if they're allowed to assume a more natural shape and are left to produce flowers and fruit. They may still need to be trimmed occasionally, but over time you may be able to turn them into a true hedgerow with a mixture of species.

Favor Natives, Enjoy Exotics

Although native plants are most often preferable, there is no need to automatically remove all exotics. This is a garden, after all—intended in part to please the gardener, and many exotics are popular with wildlife too. But any highly invasive species should be removed. In Florida, for instance, Brazilian pepper, melaleuca and Australian pine are big problems. State agencies have lists of such

Adding some feeders, a birdbath and perches to an existing garden may be all that's needed to create a miniature wildlife refuge.

plants to help gardeners know which ones to avoid.

Your space need not be large—an odd corner and your imagination can work wonders.

EVALUATING PLANTS

When choosing plants for wildlife habitat consider them by size and growth habit: big trees, smaller trees, shrubs, vines, perennials and annuals, grasses, ground covers and water plants. The guidelines on the following pages, although they do name some of the most important species in each group, are not intended as a list of recommended plants. Rather, they will give you an idea of how to evaluate plants for wildlife use. Each ecoregion has its own plants adapted to specific climates, soil and elevations. For more specific recommendations consult one of the lists published by state and local agencies and other organizations.

Familiarity with scientific names can help. Many of the plants mentioned, especially among the trees, are by the group botanists call genus. The oak genus, for example, is Quercus. Within that group are many species, which are given a second name. White oaks are thus Quercus alba, southern live oaks are Q. virginiana, valley oaks of California are Q. lobata. Knowing that oaks are among the best wildlife food plants, you can then find which species are best for your garden.

A garden that provides a wide range of plants such as this one, with zinnias, impatiens, daylilies and annual salvia, will attract an even greater range of wildlife.

TREES: THE CENTER OF THE GARDEN

Deciduous trees like maples change dramatically through the seasons, offering sweet sap and pollen-rich flowers in spring, nutritious seeds a little later, dense cover in summer, a protective soil blanket when the leaves drop in fall, and perching places in winter.

Conifers, or needle-leaved trees like the Sitka spruce, along with firs, pines, hemlocks and yews, are especially valuable for the dense year-round cover they provide.

Large trees are the backbone of the wildlife garden. They are whole ecosystems in themselves. Go right up to any good-sized tree and take a close look. Each one is distinctive, with bark that may be smooth like a beech, furrowed like an oak, or peeling up in great slabs, like that of a shagbark hickory. Different kinds of insects and microorganisms inhabit each species.

The branches vary—some thick and burly, others slender and twiggy. Leaves come in every shape, size and thickness and feed a multitude of insects that attract birds and other carnivores. Leaves also filter light and make a cooler, shadier micro-climate under the tree canopy. The sap rising from the roots is also food, brought to the surface wherever there are wounds or holes drilled by woodpeckers. Buds, catkins, nuts, cones, fruits and seeds attract hungry birds and mammals. As parts of the tree die, or become hollow, they provide homes for nesting songbirds, squirrels and owls.

Selecting Tree Species

An important distinction among trees is between conifers (needle-leaved trees) and the broadleaf trees.

Most needle-leaved trees—pines, cedars, firs, spruces and hemlocks—are great for year-round cover because they are evergreens. A few, like larches and bald cypress, shed their leaves each year. Conifers have inconspicuous wind-pollinated flowers that produce nutritious seeds borne in cones, a popular wildlife food. There are exceptions to this. Yews produce a berry-like fruit, and eastern red cedars bear a deep blue, berry-filled cone, which is loved by cedar waxwings.

In a national study of wildlife food plants, pines and oaks turned out to be among the most valuable. Both groups are highly varied, with species adapted to everything from high latitude cold regions to the steaming south, wet and dry situations, high and low elevations and a range of soil conditions.

Other especially valuable food sources for wildlife include: beech, maple, black cherry and hemlock in the northeast; hickory, hackberry, blackgum, tuliptree, ash and sweetgum in the Southeast; and pine, oak, hackberry and cherry in the prairie region. The mountain and desert regions support hackberry and maple, and also Douglas fir, willow and spruce.

In the desert southwest, the giant saguaro cactus substitutes for large old trees.

SMALLER TREES

Blooming fruit trees in spring are alive with pollinating insects, and birds soon follow; some, like cedar waxwings, nibble at blossoms.

Smaller trees create an important layering effect in the wildlife garden, filling in spaces below the tallest trees to make a transition to lower levels. On small properties in particular, planting several small trees rather than one large one can be better since they add diversity.

Birches, crabapples, hawthorne, cherries, plums, hollies and mountain ash are good choices for the wildlife garden. All produce fruits and seeds that birds and many other animals eat. When these small trees flower, they attract insects which bring in many birds, including warblers, chickadees, phoebes and kingbirds. Fallen fruits also draw insects, which in turn feed jumping mice, deer mice, ground feeding birds such as white-throated sparrows and lizards.

Crabapples are among the small trees recommended in the wildlife garden to fill in around larger species.

Crabapples are perfect hedgerow plants.

SHRUBS

Although they don't garner much attention in nursery catalogs, this group of plants is among the most important for wildlife, providing both shelter and food.

Team Them Up

The best way to use shrubs is in groups—to fill in corners, surround trees, create island beds or link islands of cover. Don't be afraid of crowding several different kinds of shrubs together. The goal is to use them to tie the garden together and create continuous sheltered homes for wildlife, not to produce individual focal points. In a small garden, a varied group of shrubs can add enormous diversity and

year-round interest for you and the local wildlife. Once established, most shrubs don't require much attention (especially if you leave them to grow to their natural shape), so they are ideal for gardeners interested in low-maintenance plantings.

Specific Selections

Lilacs start off spring in the northern areas, attracting the earliest butterflies, including the red admiral. Mulberries are among the most popular summer fruits for birds, who also love elderberries, blueberries and any of the bramble fruits like blackberries. Wild roses draw many insects while they bloom and later offer bright red

Use azaleas and other shrubs to create layers of foliage in the garden, connecting the understory with the canopy.

Common lilacs, with their sweet scent and early spring blooms, provide important nectar at a lean time.

Juicy red fruits of the highbush cranberry disappear quickly as hungry birds find them.

Within the branches of this thorny rose bush, birds find safe places to nest and feed.

rose hips for the birds. Many kinds of alders, viburnums and honeysuckle also offer food and shelter, and some, like the native sumacs, hold their fruit until the following spring to feed returning migrant birds.

In the Pacific northwest, gooseberries and snowberries are good additions. In the southwest, sagebrush, salt-bush, acacias and prickly pear are among the most important shrubs. The southeast has both temperate and tropical plants, especially in the coastal areas, including palmettos and ever-green palms that provide excellent cover.

When selecting shrubs for the wildlife garden, check to make sure they are not sterile or have enormous doubled flowers. Sterile mulberries, for instance, may not mess up the lawn with their fruits, but they also won't attract northern ori-oles or scarlet tanagers that especially love the fruit. On the other hand, it's best to put such a plant in a spot where the fruits won't cause damage. Mulberries, for instance, can stain anything they touch.

Sometime birds scatter so many berries (of all kinds) as they eat that they inadvertently help start new plants; it's possible to add more plants to the garden by simply leaving any sprouted seedlings wherever they take root.

Held conveniently above the leaves, sumac fruits keep over winter to furnish food for returning spring migrants.

FLOWERS

Traditional English perennial borders are a great model for the wildlife garden.

Echinacea.

One of the great things about wildlife gardening is that flowers are essential. A wide range of colorful beds, offering scented blooms throughout the growing season, is one of the best ways to maintain a diverse and vibrant community of animals. Flowers offer nectar and pollen for insects, which in turn feed birds, reptiles, amphibians and small mammals.

Flower seeds also feed a wide range of animals and birds, and hidden in the foliage is a lively community of invertebrates busily decomposing plant parts and eating each other.

A Good Example

Old-fashioned, informal cottage gardens are great models for the wildlife garden. A mixture of annuals and perennials with a sprinkling of herbs, vegetables and weeds is ideal since it provides a variety of plant heights, bloom times and a range of colors and shapes. Such gardens "hum" with pollinators and draw a steady supply of butterflies and birds. Cottage gardens are complex places, far more interesting than rows of per-

fectly arranged specimens. And the old-fashioned varieties of garden flowers with single blooms are the best choices because they are more recognizable to insect visitors. It doesn't mean giving up favorite hybrids; just mix them with other flowers for best results.

Flower Basics

Many of the standard garden flowers attract wildlife, among them petunias, marigolds, asters, ageratum and sunflowers; chapter 6 lists some of those especially popular with butterflies and hummingbirds.

Rudbeckia.

Goldenrod.

Sunflower.

The overall goal is to have continuous blooming and diversity in the garden. One way to accomplish this is to have representatives of different plant families. With some practice, you can learn to identify the characteristics of each family and this will add another level to your understanding of the plant world.

Beebalm, a member of the mint family and popular with hummingbirds and butterflies, also comes in other colors.

Composites (Asters)

A few plant families are musts. One group is the composite or aster family. Plants in this group have flowers clustered together in a head. In many, the outside ring of flowers sports a single petal so the whole arrangement looks like a single flower; daisies are the classic example.

Composites are great for foraging insects because each little flower contains nectar that is easy to reach and the flowers are packed together, offering a convenient landing site and plenty of food in one spot. Stop and look at the surface of a developing sunflower head sometime and you'll be amazed at the activity there. Even before it has fully opened, insects are coming to check it out.

Other members of the composite family are rudbeckia, pur-

ple coneflower, yarrow, gaillardia and asters. The weedy members of this family, as popular with wildlife as they are unpopular with gardeners, are goldenrods, thistles and ragweeds.

Mints

Mints are in another large family that includes many familiar garden flowers. Beebalm, salvias, lavender, mints, rosemary and self-heal are just a few examples of this family, and most are very popular with butterflies.

Parsley Family

The plants with flowers in umbels like Queen Anne's lace, dill and fennel, are especially

Queen Anne's lace blends easily with ornamentals in the perennial border.

important as larval plants for some butterflies, and because they attract beneficial insects that help keep pests in check.

Constant Bloom

The overall strategy of keeping constant bloom in the garden takes a while to work out since conditions vary so much. Experienced wildlife gardeners have learned to include wildflowers in their annual cycle of blooms, as well as weedy species that more fastidious gardeners would remove. Purple-flowered self-heal left to bloom in the lawn is a good example, as is the occasional mullein and Queen Anne's lace left in the perennial bed. Native flowers will bring in butterflies and other pollinators, and in some cases are necessary for the survival of these visitors.

Flowers attract insects, which in turn bring the birds, reptiles, amphibians and small mammals to the garden.

Gaillardia.

VINES

Native Virginia creeper reaches high into the tree canopy, and turns brilliant red in fall to signal birds that the dark fruits are ripe.

Vines are great connectors, linking ground and canopy, and trees within forest or groves. Vines are among the most versatile plants, since they can be allowed to grow wild to create a safe tangle for wildlife, or trained tamely on a wall to become a source of food for birds and insects. A dead tree can "live" again with a climbing vine planted at its base. Perennial vines are a year-round long-term asset, while annual flowering vines like scarlet runner beans can be used to quickly create separate "rooms" in the garden.

Choosing Vines

When choosing vines, consider the flowers, the fruits and how aggressive the plants are in your area. While some—like grapes—may be safely grown on trees, a few, including English ivy, can become serious problems and choke out their host.

Wild-growing vines can be appropri-

Vigorous vines like honeysuckle will quickly cover a stump, creating more habitat and shelter for wildlife.

ated to be part of the wildlife garden. One side of Steve Parren's garden, for example, is bordered by a mass of wild grapes that have grown up into tall trees at the edge of the forest. One summer day he saw a bluebird that was being chased by a kestrel dash for cover among the vines. He could then hear the bluebird taunting the frustrated hawk from within the safe cover of the grapevines. In the fall, the vines turn bright colors from the Virginia creeper mixed in,

Red flowers of trumpet creeper attract hummingbirds.

making a gorgeous backdrop for the garden and feeding flocks of birds.

Other perennial vines of great value to wildlife are Dutchman's pipe, a favorite of swallowtail butterflies, and trumpet creeper, which hummingbirds love. Even poison ivy and poison oak have their merits, since their berries are an important food source for birds in much of North America.

Beware the three-part shiny leaves of poison ivy. Birds love the fruits and spread the seeds of this tenacious, irritating climber all over.

GRASSES

Grasses are one of the most adaptable and widespread plant families. Grasses are an essential ingredient of meadows and prairies since their roots help create a stable environment below ground, and above ground the leaves and seed heads provide food, cover and nesting material for all kinds of wildlife. Humans also depend on grasses—corn, wheat, rye and rice are all members of this plant family.

An Essential for Birds

Some of the birds most dependent on grass seed are ducks, red-winged blackbirds, bobolinks, cardinals, grosbeaks, longspurs, sparrows, buntings and meadowlarks. Crabgrass, so dreaded as an agricultural and garden weed, is eaten by many songbirds, including sparrows, juncos and mourning doves;

even turkeys eat it. Other animals that depend on grass seed include ground-dwelling mammals like pocket mice and ground squirrels.

Standard Grass—A Desert

Many lawn grasses are kept short and unproductive so they provide none of these advantages for wildlife. Most are turf-forming, meaning they spread sideways and form a dense, shallow mat of roots that doesn't leave much room for other plants and tends to shed a lot of water. Their favorite growing seasons are spring and fall, when conditions are cooler, like in their homelands in northern Europe. Midsummer finds them thirsty and miserable, and often requiring lots of attention and resources in

most of North America's hotter climates.

Native Grass—A Garden

In contrast to turf grass, some of our native grasses are clumping species. Instead of spreading horizontally, they make discrete fountain-like clumps, with space between them. Water can penetrate the soil much more easily, and other plants can grow between the clumps. Species like little bluestem, for instance, are perfect companions for deeper rooted perennials typical of prairies and meadows.

Some warm-season grass species are adapted to hot summers. They start growth later and grow happily during summer's heat, flowering and producing seed heads in fall when they turn various shades of brown, russet and gold. They range in height from less than a foot to much more, like the stately big bluestem that can reach 10 feet in height.

Species suitable for the wildlife garden include panicgrass or switchgrass, brome grass, prairie dropseed and buffalo grass. Some of the ornamental grasses that hold their seeds for long periods can also be a valuable food reserve in winter.

The grass family is among the most important of all in feeding and sheltering animals.

GROUNDCOVERS

Groundcovers make valuable additions to the wildlife garden. They cover the ground neatly without having to be mowed, and many bloom or produce fruit that is attractive to a variety of wildlife. Under trees in shady areas especially,

Look for native plants in your region to incorporate as groundcovers along paths.

Ostrich ferns and pachysandra carpet the ground under trees, protecting soil organisms and ground dwellers, and minimizing upkeep.

they make a lot more sense than grass, which needs a lot of sunlight to grow well.

In wooded and partly sunny areas, lamium, wintergreen, sweet woodruff and wild ginger are possibilities. If moss begins to take over, let it; after a while there will be much less mowing for you to do. Ferns, although they don't provide much food for animals, do make great cover and their fronds and the hairy covering of buds are used by some birds in constructing nests. There are many choices, from the low-growing evergreen Christmas fern to the delicate maidenhair fern.

PLANTING PATTERNS

Wildlife gardens use designs and planting patterns similar to those of conventional gardens, but always with the needs of wildlife in mind as well. Usually, this means there's a more relaxed attitude about what goes where, and the arrangement of specific garden features may cater more to the needs of wildlife than the pleasures of the human eye. What's lost in tradition is more than made up for in the colors and activity of birds, butterflies and other wildlife that are attracted. On the following pages are examples of plant groupings that work, taken from real gardens, to suggest how to go about planning your plantings.

A garden that considers wildlife takes on a relaxed and comfortable look all its own.

PERENNIAL BEDS

A perennial bed can incorporate small trees like this Kousa dogwood; note how this bed fills the corner, then continues to sweep along the fence instead of ending abruptly.

When planning or expanding perennial beds, don't think of them as just isolated square or rectangular shapes stuck in the middle of a lawn. Rather, make them part of the overall movement of the garden—stopping places for butterflies, hummingbirds and other creatures.

A Good Example

The Parrens have worked at this over the years, gradually chipping away at the lawn that was originally all they had. On the north side of their house is a bed of hostas and astilbe, a rich pattern of varied leaf shapes and textures with shades of white and pink feathery flowers. It is a favorite area for toads to hang out, and the chipmunks use it as part of their travel route around the house. In fact, the Parrens have often observed all kinds small creatures run and hide under the sheltering, low-growing leaves.

Right around the corner, by the back doorway, is another bed filled with ferns and a mixture of other plant species. Not as manicured as the hosta bed, it provides important cover for a variety of wildlife, including butterfly larvae.

In front of the house, facing south, are two beds; one warms up in early spring and features bulbs and the other comes into full flower in fall. Late spring and summer is when a long curving bed in back is most colorful and varied; it wraps around the gazebo and partially hides it from view, making it a perfect observation area for wildlife. Butterflies, other insects and hummingbirds are active all day, and once the flowers fade, goldfinches begin their acrobatic harvesting of seeds left to mature.

You Can Mix Approaches

Lauren and Steve each take different approaches to gardening. She enjoys fussing over each new plant, while he tends to focus on how all the plantings flow together so they benefit wildlife. Between them, they've managed to create a beautiful garden filled with flowers that bloom constantly and provide shelter and food for a variety of wildlife.

ISLAND BED

Although planned mostly for aesthetics, English style country gardens, with their many layers, diverse plantings and meandering paths, often become refuges for birds and other wildlife.

assorted heights. Include both evergreen and deciduous species, along with some fruiting shrubs for birds. Then see what happens. Birds will bring in more plant species, the wind will add others and squirrels or jays may plant nuts and seeds there, too. If you allow annuals and perennials to colonize the edges, you may find a rich butterfly habitat developing over time. One island bed could be left to grow and connect with others, helping to break up the lawn and draw in more wildlife.

The Parren's garden provides a good example of how island beds can develop. Steve started an island bed with a basswood, hemlock and apple tree planted about 6 or 7 feet apart. Over time, a birch and sumac joined the group, as well as a weigela and a rose that was a gift from a neighbor. The island is now substantial, with plenty of protected space for nesting birds and several other regular residents.

A bold way to break up a large, open lawn is to make an island bed with trees and shrubs, as well as perennials, vines and annuals if you want. The best way to try out this idea is to take a garden hose and lay it out where you think you might want to put the bed. You may want to place the bed so that it conceals something you don't want to look at, or simply adds some intrigue to an area. On the other hand, be sure to check that the island bed won't block a view you like once the plants have matured.

Creating the Bed

Once you've chosen a location and shape for your island bed, it's time to clear the lawn from the area. This may involve removing large areas of sod, or simply digging holes for individual plants and smothering the grass around them with a deep layer of mulch. As the plants grow they will shade the area enough that the grass will eventually die out.

Vary the Plants

Choose a variety of plants for the bed, using species with

HEDGEROW

When planting a hedgerow in the wildlife garden, the goal is to create a relatively tangled area of continuous cover, so 3 or 4 feet between some plants is fine. Another approach is to put them farther apart and allow others to fill in. This requires some monitoring since birds bring not only desirable plants like mulberry or cherry, but also invasives you don't want.

Managing the Hedgerow

Managing a hedgerow means getting to know the plants so that you can remove potential problems. Large trees like water oaks will need to come out before they overwhelm other plants.

Steve Parren started a hedgerow along his driveway to form a windbreak and cover for animals. He began by transplanting a lot of white pine seedlings, and during the 10 years they've been maturing, he has also encouraged the growth of chokecherries and sumac that birds have brought in to the area. "Often it's a matter of knowing what not to cut," he says.

Let Them Grow

Bill Fontenot, who has a native plant nursery in Louisiana, is another fan of hedgerows. He says the wider the hedgerow the better, even up to 20 feet. He suggests starting with small trees planted in the center. In the southeast, for example, good choices would be American holly, Carolina buckthorn, Indian cherry, swamp or roughleaved dogwood, hackberry or sassafras. In the north, try crabapples, Russian olive (it's not fancy but wildlife love it) or fruit trees.

You could then build in both directions with large shrubs like viburnums, yaupon or cassine holly and swamp rose. In front of these add smaller shrubs like snowberry, antique roses, American beautyberry and native lantana. An edging of beebalm, purple coneflower, Joe Pye weed and many other annuals and perennials, will attract butterflies.

A border of brambles and conifers forms an informal hedgerow.

MEADOWS AND PRAIRIES

The interest in wildflowers and meadows has unfortunately led to some misconceptions. For instance the widely sold "meadow in a can" seed mixtures suggest that all it takes to create this kind of plant community is to sprinkle some seeds around. This approach overlooks the beauty and complexity that comprise the true meadow and prairie environments.

Prairie or Meadow?

One might begin by asking whether meadows and prairies are in fact the same thing. Neil Diboll is owner of Prairie Nursery, a midwest company that specializes in prairie plants. He explains the difference:

Both meadows and prairies are plant communities of grasses and flowers, but prairies are in the midwest and include warm season grasses (like little bluestem and switchgrass) and only native flowers. Meadows, or eastern meadows as they are often called, are in the east and can have naturalized non-native flowers along with the natives. If they have only natives, they are called native eastern meadows.

Many of the same plants grow in meadows and prairies, and there once were stands of very tall grasslands as far east as Long Island that clearly were an extension of the midwestern prairie. In Louisiana there were once extensive prairies, too. Western grasslands are often referred to as prairies; high mountain grasslands are called alpine meadows. The distinction between prairies and meadows then, is one created by people. But then, the name "prairie" is

Poppies and bachelor's buttons often mark the first year of common wildflower mixes that are soon crowded out by weedy invaders. A long-lasting meadow planting requires good soil preparation and a mixture of grasses and flowers appropriate to the area.

Wildflower meadows are eventually invaded by woody species; to keep that from happening, they must periodically be cut, mowed or burned.

derived from the French word for meadow, so why argue?

Each stand of prairie or meadow is a distinct community, with different proportions of grass and forbs and different species dominating. It's a result of which seeds blew in, how long the site has been established, the water supply and when the site was last burned, mowed or grazed. These variables are what make meadows and prairies so interesting. No matter what you start with, it will inevitably change through the years.

Starting a Prairie or Meadow

Starting a true prairie or meadow planting is a lot like starting a perennial garden. First you take out everything that's there, then you plant. When you get ready to put in a prairie planting, look for a mix appropriate to your region and soil type. Some plants deal more effectively with clay, for instance, while others are suited to wet, dry or sandy locations.

It's a lot of work at first, weeding and caring for the new plants, but once they are established, care will be minimal.

Depending on where you are and what exactly you plant, upkeep will be occasional mowing or burning. As with perennials, a good idea is to start with a small patch, using transplants. For larger areas, seeding results in a better stand of prairie. Some gardeners take a mixed approach, seeding the area but adding enough transplants so that the area has some blooms the first and second years. Prairie plants tend to be slow growers, so the effect is opposite of what happens with a meadow-in-a-can approach; instead of a quick burst of color the first year followed by a more and more ragged look, a true prairie or meadow starts out ragged, and gradually begins to look better each year after that.

Maintaining the Prairie or Meadow

Once established, prairies and meadows can be counted on to

supply changing colors and textures year-round. They will also become home to an astounding variety of wildlife, including animals that fly, crawl, burrow, run, leap and slither. In summer you will see lots of activity above ground, and in winter there will be all kinds of activity within the protective cover of the grass stems and underground.

Keep a Wild Patch Somewhere

Doing nothing is often the main technique to a more varied garden. If letting some wild-growing plants mix in with the cultivated flowers offends you, try leaving a wild patch somewhere else on the property. Screen it if you must. Stands of wildflowers can be beautiful and will also provide home for butterflies. Eastern black swallowtails, for example, feed on phlox and milkweed, while the larva feeds on plants of the carrot family such as parsley, celery and wild Queen Anne's lace.

MAINTAINING THE WILDLIFE GARDEN

The Concept of Succession

In thinking about the wildlife garden, it helps to understand the process ecologists call succession.

Whenever there is bare soil available, a predictable set of stages begins. Annual plants that love disturbed soil and thrive in full sun colonize it. They are followed by longer-

lived perennials that get started in the protection of the annuals. Eventually, as the perennials become established, they crowd out the colonizers. Shrubs and trees get their footholds and as they mature, there is less light at ground level so only shade-lovers manage to get started.

Eventually a community of long-lived species, usually dominated by woody plants, matures. When one of these large plants falls down, or if fire or flood disturbs the community, the pioneer plants have a chance to grow again. Each ecoregion has its own species of plants and animals that are typical to these different stages of succession. In some areas tall trees dominate in the later stages, in others it is small perennials.

Allow Succession to Occur

Most gardens do not permit the natural cycles of succession to occur. The vegetable patch, which could be a paradise for weedy, sun-loving annuals and perennials, is tilled every year. The grasses in the lawn are kept immature, so they never flower or set seed. And gardeners wage constant war on other sun-loving species that try to invade the lawn area. Even the growth under and around trees is cleared out so hedges, vines, shrubs and groundcovers can no longer thrive in such places. No wonder it takes a lot of work to maintain the whole place.

To create a garden that is easy to maintain and that wildlife loves, the main technique is to find ways to cooperate with the natural cycle of things. Encourage areas of the garden to replicate different stages of succession. The greater the variety of habitats or successional stages you have in the garden, the more birds, animals and interesting insects you are likely to attract. Your role is to learn what is going on, to see what direction it is going and create an environment that encourages the process.

You can also save yourself a lot of money and energy by doing this. And the wildlife garden's rewards go beyond these savings; you'll soon begin to count the birds, animals and butterflies you attract as part of your natural payoff.

A garden that mixes native and non-native species is attractive to a wide range of wildlife. This garden includes purple coneflower, dianthus and coreopsis.

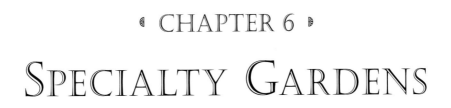

◀ CHAPTER 6 ▶
SPECIALTY GARDENS

I t's fine to say, "I have a wildlife-friendly garden," and then welcome all the various visitors you get.

But many gardeners have a special interest in a certain type of wildlife, and wish to gear at least a portion of their yard to birds, animals or insects. Different regions and situations call for different plants and strategies. That's what this chapter is all about—guiding you in deciding exactly what needs to be done, in your ecoregion, to attract birds, hummingbirds and butterflies.

You won't find specific garden plans here; designing your own garden wildlife habitat is half the fun. But what you will find are specific strategies and elements you can incorporate to attract the wildlife you're interested in.

Each wildlife garden will be different, designed to fit the location and interests of the gardener.

BIRDS

A feeder made of mesh keeps seeds dry and easily accessible.

A shallow basket holds seed for ground-feeding birds.

If you create a garden attractive to a wide variety of birds, chances are most other wildlife will be happy there, too. Feeders are only part of the strategy; more important are the plants you choose, how you arrange them, and the presence of water. The goal is a garden that has good year-round cover, places for nesting and a succession of flowers and fruits that feed the birds or attract the insects they need. The more variety in all of this, the greater the number of birds that will come. And while large rural properties might have more visitors, even a tiny urban yard or porch can offer a chance to see a succession of interesting bird species.

Stacked plastic trays with cover are easy to fill and clean and provide safety from cats.

Birdfeeders

Birdfeeders are mostly for people—providing us a look into the otherwise hidden world of birds. It is perfectly all right to leave feeders up all year. When wild foods are plentiful, seeds at feeders are strictly supplemental food. During lean times, birds may count on these free foods, so if you start feeding in fall in harsh winter areas, continue through spring. Feeders in summer aren't as busy as in the winter, since there is so much other food available; but they

do tend to keep birds nearby, and they encourage nesting species to bring their young ones. Seeing young cardinals or nuthatches arriving with their parents to learn about feeders is a rare opportunity to learn about bird parenting behavior.

In some areas of the country there are relatively few seed-eating birds, and no amount of feeding will result in the kinds of scenes northern gardeners are

Highbush cranberry is a good bird-attracting plant for midwestern gardeners.

Goldfinch on thistle seed feeder.

feeding, but it also gives the birds a much-needed resource for bathing. Try to make the water supply especially steady and reliable in drier climates, in the warm and dry seasons in cooler climates, and during winter.

Bird Migration

Birds follow a few main paths when moving north and south each year. Part of the fun of bird gardening is becoming attuned to seasons by what the birds are doing, who's out there nesting or passing through. Major flyways follow river valleys like the Mississippi and its tributaries, as well as mountain ranges (either side of the Appalachians and Rockies) and

A simple plastic tube feeder.

both seacoasts. The prairie states also have a flyway. A well planned yard, with plenty of food, water and roosting sites, can become a regular stopping place along these routes.

used to. In southern Louisiana, for example, Bill Fontenot puts out millet only to lure painted buntings where he can see them. The secret to abundant birdlife around the house is in the plantings and reliable water sources.

In the end, though, that's the secret anywhere—habitat. The most expensive feeder in the world, filled with high-cost seed, won't attract many if any worthwhile birds. North, south, east or west, what you plant is key. As you'll see in the case studies to come, for attracting birds the focus should always be on native plants that will bring birds into the yard. Once there, they will find your feeders.

Don't forget water, and don't entrust it to your own human neighbors to supply. Water can be one of the most critical elements for birds year round, and it will really attract them to, and hold them in, your yard. Providing water is a form of

Put some feeders in more secluded spots for shy birds.

NORTHEAST AND MIDWEST

A hummingbird feeder hangs from a nesting box.

American goldfinch, thistle eater extraordinaire, bright in his yellow summer finery.

Steve Parren's garden is a great example of how to make birds feel at home and safe. In the center of a modest lawn is a complete feeding station. At times the number and variety of birds eating is hardly believable, and the colors enough to overwhelm even a long-time birdwatcher—goldfinches, rosebreasted grosbeaks, cardinals, bluejays, downy and hairy woodpeckers are all present. But while the feeding station (which offers a variety of food throughout the year) is where they see the birds, the real secret to attracting them is in the whole garden setting.

The open lawn around the feeder gives birds a good view of potential dangers. No cats can scale the pole, so birds are safe from below. If kestrels or other hawks threaten from above, tangles of wild grapevines nearby offer shelter. A young butternut tree growing near the porch and feeder is popular as a waiting and look out area. Ground feeding birds and chipmunks feel safe below the feeder since

A male northern cardinal helps make up for the lack of flowers in winter.

Northeast and Midwest Bird Plants
(listed in order of ripening)

Juneberry	*Amelanchier* spp.
Elderberry	*Sambucus* spp., especially *S. canadensis*
Mulberry	*Morus alba, Morus rubra*
Brambles	*Rubus* spp.
Viburnums	*Viburnum* spp.
Wild grapes	*Vitis labrusca*
Honeysuckle	*Lonicera* spp.
Dogwood	*Cornus* spp.

Wild grapes.

Honeysuckle.

Red elderberry.

Flowering dogwood.

Bluebird.

there are nearby shrubs and perennial plantings.

The Parrens manage their gardens so that birds can find food on their own among the plantings. Native and exotic species are blended, allowing the birds to be part of the planting and design. In the hedgerow Steve has started as a screen along the drive, birds have added wild cherries and sumac. The perennial bed in back features a native shadbush, chosen for its earliest spring blooms so welcome by pollinators; catbirds snap up the early summer fruits while they're still green. Mullein has made itself a place in the perennial bed, attracting insect-loving nuthatches, and later chickadees to its seeds. All the perennials are left to develop seedheads, many of which last through the winter and are consumed by the many goldfinches that live here all year.

All along the garden edge, to help it blend into the wild, vines like the grapes and Virginia creeper grow unchecked into neighboring trees. Brambles of various kinds also make a great safety zone and add important fruit during the summer; it requires occasional weeding to keep them from overwhelming the perennials, but is well worth the time for its benefits to wildlife.

At one end of the garden, Steve has allowed a patch of sumac to grow. The brilliant red candles of fruit (held above yellow fall foliage) are breathtaking, and even more colorful when bluebirds stop to feast on them in early spring when they return, hungry, from the south.

Nesting sites are plentiful among the trees and shrubs and Steve has added nesting boxes, which are used by bluebirds, tree swallows and the occasional flying squirrel.

The birds find water in simple birdbaths, one on the ground by the perennials, one in the middle of the lawn, and a small plastic-lined pool in the shade. In winter, one bath is kept thawed with a simple heater.

Essentials for birds are all available within a compact area. Accustomed to the family being there, rose-breasted grosbeaks feed, unconcerned, as do goldfinches, nuthatches and various woodpeckers. Some practically become family members, like Baby Hughey, a fat downy woodpecker that spent a whole weekend begging for suet from any black and white bird that showed up after his mother stopped feeding him.

Nesting boxes take the place of hollows in decaying trees.

Common mullein produces seeds that chickadees love.

DESERT, SOUTHWEST

In desert regions of the southwest, prickly pear cactus provides excellent cover and food for animals.

Some birds, like wrens, will nest on simple open shelves mounted on walls.

In drier regions, tall trees and vines are rare; birds find cover among small trees, shrubs and

Gila woodpecker atop a blooming saguaro cactus.

rocks. The most common landscape style in this region is a square of lawn, watered twice a day. Not much there for birds.

But Barbara Penelle found that when she planted native desert species, she immediately began to see many more birds on her property. No colorful cardinals or goldfinches brighten her feeders; desert species are more subdued in coloration. But the towhees are spectacular, she says, and

many of birds have their own distinctive characters and personalitites. In fact, she and her husband have become so involved with the wildlife on their plot that they purchased the lot next door to keep it from being developed.

She's had to figure out about wildlife and gardening in the arid southwest. Nobody could tell her about how often to water native

Killdeer are strictly meat-eaters.

A Costa's hummingbird feeding on ocotillo.

plants once they were put in her yard, so she's learned by experience. When they got rid of the lawn and other water loving plants, even though they added a pool at the same time, the Penelles did find that their water bill dropped to one-third of its previous level. She now uses only soaker or drip irrigation. Many of the new plants, like desert marigold and the cacti, don't need extra water at all.

Feeding birds was also a mystery—most available information concerned the standard garden birds of the north and east. When Barbara first put out birdseed, the house was overrun with pigeons, sometimes 100 of them on the roof. Finally, she figured out most of the desert birds like thistle seed, but the pigeons don't, so that's all she puts out now. There

are feeders all over the yard, mostly open trays placed on walls. She doesn't have to worry about rain or about squirrels stealing seed—all she has is ground squirrels, and they get peanuts.

Sparrows, house finches, lesser goldfinches, mockingbirds, western meadowlarks, verdins and doves are year round residents. In winter, migrants like red-winged blackbirds, flickers and towhees join in. Starlings pass by but don't stop. She has two kinds of hummingbirds: Anna's in winter and black-chinned in summer.

Barbara laughs as she admits to how completely she's

become involved with the birds. During the winter, she leaves little caches of mealworms under the many rocks, so she can watch rock wrens scurry around looking for them. One winter she helped a one-legged killdeer survive. She had to buy three different books to find out that what it would eat; finally she learned it eats meat and was able to supply it with mealworms. Her daughter got so attached to the bird when she took care of the house for a while that she would come to visit for weeks afterward. The bird finally moved on. One year Barbara even bought a small aviary for an injured woodpecker she wanted to save.

Nesting boxes were a learning experience, too. Wanting to provide home for as many species as possible, she bought a whole assortment of boxes from a local branch of a national chainstore that offers bird supplies. Among them was

Purchase ocotillo (right) and other desert plants from reputable nurseries that don't dig them up in the wild.

Cholla and barrel cactus surrounded by spring flowers are just a few of the many beautiful native species available for gardeners wishing to attract desert wildlife.

Prickly Pear.

Holes excavated in saguaro by gila woodpeckers become nesting sites for other animals.

an expensive flicker box her husband mounted high up on the pool house. But no birds came to occupy the boxes. Finally she learned why—the species that used them don't nest in her area, but move north for breeding season. The lesson: Learn about nesting patterns of birds in your area before adding nest boxes, and don't be fooled by what's available in stores.

Her husband totally mystified the neighbors with his project on the recently purchased lot next door. To provide places for birds to perch and

hide (until they are able to plant), he covered the area with branches dragged there from vacant lots all over the neighborhood.

Plants especially valuable for cover and food in the desert southwest are mesquite, palo verde, rabbitbrush, acacia, creosote, brittlebush, prickly pear, Joshua tree, barrel cactus and desert willow. Barbara also has Mexican redbud, ocotillo, mescal bean tree, bursage and a number of salvias. A plant seldom mentioned in lists for the region is *Salvia greggii*, which she believes to be the absolute favorite of hummingbirds.

Southwest Bird Plants

Desert Plants

Utah serviceberry	*Amelanchier utahensis*
(example of regional variation of species of useful genus)	
Squawbush sumac	*Rhus trilobata*
Shrub live oak	*Quercus turbinella*
Utah juniper	*Juniperus osteosperma*

Mountain and Valley Plants

Dwarf mountain ash	*Sorbus scopulina*
Blue elderberry	*Sambucus caerulea*
Utah honeysuckle	*Lonicera utahensis*

BIRDFEEDERS AND SQUIRRELS

A suspending feeder is one solution to squirrel problems, though it works only in a place where there are no overhanging trees from which squirrels can jump. Among the feeders should be one that offers niger seed, favored by the smaller birds like goldfinches, and one with sunflower seeds for a wide range of species including chickadees, cardinals, grosbeaks, nuthatches and many others. Suet is especially valued in winter, though some birds continue to take it into summer. Suet attracts members of the woodpecker family that don't otherwise frequent feeders. Oranges impaled on wooden spikes attract orioles in early spring.

One solution to squirrel problems: Suspend feeders from wire and cover them with squirrel guards.

SOUTH, SOUTHEAST

In southern Louisiana, Bill Fontenot says there are so few seed-eating birds that he has a feeder only to be able to see painted buntings up close. The best way to have a lot of birds around the house there is to focus on habitat, he says. Dense plantings that focus on fruiting shrubs and lots of cover, with many layers of vegetation, will draw many species.

Insects are what the birds depend on most, so pesticides must be avoided. The sound of water dripping will bring birds in, too, and will also attract migrants during the great spring and fall migrations.

Shrubs are important in this region. Among the most important for birds are blueberries, huckleberries, cherries and the many species of hollies.

Within the south are many distinctly different ecological systems, including the sand plains along the coast, live oak forests and hammocks, pine forest, mixed hardwood forests, tall gallery forests along the rivers, great swamps and a few remnants of native prairie. Tropical and temperate species mix, so the opportunities and choices for gardeners are remarkable.

Although to northern gardeners the seasons may seem relatively unchanging, migrating birds make for distinctly different seasons. As you get inland from the coasts as well as higher in elevation, you will begin to find seed-eating birds, so don't ignore feeders entirely.

Flowering cherries.

A succession of fruit-bearing shrubs is key to keeping birds in the garden. Huckleberry is one good choice; always look for locally adapted varieties.

South, Southeast Bird Plants

Shrubs

Privet	*Ligustrum* spp.
Blackberry	*Rubus* spp.
Blueberry	*Vaccinium ashei* cultivars
Elderberry	*Sambucus* spp.
Sassafras	*Sassafras albidum*
Florida trema	*Trema guineensis*
Pokeweed	*Phytolacca americana*
American beautyberry	*Callicarpa* spp.
Spicebush	*Calycanthus* spp.
Viburnum	*Viburnum* spp.
Wax myrtle	*Myrica cerifera*

Trees

Red mulberry	*Morus rubra*
Black cherry	*Prunus serotina*
Dogwoods	*Cornus florida, Cornus kousa*
Holly	*Ilex* spp.
Cherry laurel	*Prunus caroliniana*

Viburnum dentatum.

Blackberry.

Viburnum.

Highbush blueberry.

PACIFIC NORTHWEST

When Ann and Eric Wilson renovated their small urban lot in Portland, Oregon, their main goal was to replace the square of grass that looked like a volleyball court with native plants. They spend a lot of time hiking and thought it would be great to have some of the plant species they saw in the wild, represented right at home. They have created an area that gives them a place to raise some vegetables and fruits, room to barbeque and entertain friends and host quite a few birds. Their yard is another recogized as a wildlife habitat by the NWF.

The Wilsons' strategy, one that would help make any yard attractive to birds, was to focus their own activities right by the house, and turn the edges into protected habitat. Raised beds around a tiny lawn and a sitting area make sure the couple can easily see the plants. Large native mahonia makes a great hedge and backdrop along the back fence. Its prickly, shiny, evergreen leaves create shelter for birds, and the blue berries are both decorative and a good

food source. In front of the mahonia are native vine maples that grow 10 feet tall. The final layer is shrubs: huckleberries, salal and blueberries (not native) and one crabapple. The Wilsons share the blueberries with robins and jays. Native and exotic perennials add color.

The honeysuckle vine growing on a fence attracts hummingbirds, and once they found a wren nest within its tangles. In the annual garden they also plant some of the smaller sunflower varieties, tying them up at the end of the season so the birds can harvest them on their own through fall and winter.

Landscaping with native plants is popular in the Northwest, where books and articles on the topic are common and where landowners are being encouraged to cut down on lawns. In spite of its reputation for being always rainy, July and August can be hot and dry.

Many of the Wilsons' plants came from a nursery that specializes in rescuing plants from

Tie up sunflowers at the end of the season so birds can do the harvesting.

areas being logged or developed. "Wood orphans," they call them. These plants are much less costly than the usual landscape choices, a definite advan-

Pacific Region Bird Plants

Mahonia	*Mahonia* spp.
Salal	*Gaultheria shallon*
Native huckleberries	*Vaccinium* spp.
Blueberries	*Vaccinium angustifolium*
Currants	*Ribes* spp.
Viburnums	*Viburnum* spp.
Serviceberry	*Amelanchier alnifolia*
Winterberry	*Ilex verticillata*
Mountain ash	*Sorbus* spp.

Crabapples are staples in a wildlife garden. From spring flowering through the fall crop they provide food, shelter and nesting sites.

Both seed and insect eating birds will find plenty to keep them happy in this garden, planned around a sitting area where the owners can sit and enjoy their visitors.

tage since they had to put in many plants.

A good decision in such a small urban area, where cats are common, was not to add nesting boxes. The bird bath is 30 inches high, also reducing cat danger. When the water is deep, robins and jays splash around in it; the smaller birds like sparrows follow as it gets shallower. Ann says in winter, if she regularly removes the ice, birds are there all the time.

A suet feeder brought some new visitors. First came a ruby-crowned kinglet, then a flock of bushtits began to show up every morning and evening.

Birds especially welcome suet during cold seasons. Suet will bring in woodpeckers.

BIRD HOUSES

Purple martin houses come in many shapes and sizes; martins insist on being near open areas and preferably water.

Bird nesting boxes are designed for cavity nesters: bluebirds, chickadees, nuthatches, titmice, woodpeckers, flycatchers, flickers and barn and screech owls.

Naturalists discourage you from putting up nesting boxes unless you are prepared to monitor them. Thousands are put up each year with good intentions, and many simply become another place for invasive species like house sparrows and starlings to multiply. These birds throw out native birds, often killing the young, and can raise several broods a year, thus increasing competition for space. Not many gardeners are prepared to kill young birds, or even destroy the eggs; most of the time the better solution is to concentrate on providing natural places for nesting, where native species have a better chance of competing. But one of the keys to attracting the species you want is getting the entrance hole sized right. Here are a few of the preferred diameters:

Swallow	1^1/$_2$"
Bluebird	1^1/$_2$"
Downy woodpecker	1^3/$_8$"
Titmouse	1^1/$_4$"
Chickadee	1^1/$_8$"
Nuthatch	1^1/$_8$"
House wren	1^1/$_8$"

Birds living in these boxes will help with pest control.

Tree swallows and nesting box.

BIRDFEEDERS

Several kinds of seeds can be offered in this covered triple tube feeder.

Choosing a birdfeeder can be an overwhelming task. Before investing a lot of money, decide what kind of birds you would like to feed and where in the yard might be an opportune spot. A simple wooden tray for sunflower seed is sufficient if you live in an area without squirrels. In a wooded areas, one of the more elaborate feeders designed to keep seed dry and squirrels out may be more appropriate. One that seems to do the trick has a perch that is weight sensitive—you can adjust it so that anything heavier than a cardinal, for instance, will close the hopper. Tube feeders, with six to eight feeding ports, are popular and the birds seem to like them.

Offer a variety of feeders: several that hang and attract the smaller birds, a sturdy platform or covered feeder to accommodate larger or groundfeeding birds and maybe one right by the window where you can keep an eye on it. One of my favorites mounts into a second floor

Orange half on a shelf feeder will attract orioles.

A feeding station combines a variety of feeders.

window and has one-way glass so you can see the birds up close as they feed.

Check feeders regularly, clean them every couple of weeks to get rid of moldy seed and clean up the area under the feeder, too. Piles of rotting seeds and hulls can attract rats, mice and other pests. A tray under the feeder makes this easier.

Sunflower seed and niger are the two best staples to offer. Black oil sunflower seeds are especially nutritious, attracting cardinals, nuthatches, chickadees, jays, sparrows, all the finches, grosbeaks and the smaller woodpeckers.

Goldfinches, pine siskins and redpolls (winter visitors) particularly relish niger (thistle) seed. Sparrows, doves, juncos and quail like millet seed, preferably offered on the ground. Don't purchase cheap supermarket mixes; go to a bird store and get the real thing.

Offering suet will increase the

Mixed seed in a box seeder appeals to different bird species.

Screened trays catch spill from feeder, cut down on pest problems and keep seed dry for ground feeders.

variety of birds coming to eat, including woodpeckers that normally don't come to feeders, nuthatches and chickadees.

Designer bird feeder with thatched roof adds a decorative element to garden.

HUMMINGBIRD GARDEN

Red flowers attract hummingbirds, but once in the garden, hummers will visit others in search of nectar and insects.

Big, bright hibiscus flowers will catch hummingbirds' attention.

Hummingbirds must be the most popular birds in North America. Even people who don't garden put out feeders for hummers, and just about everyone has heard that hummingbirds like red tubular flowers. They do, of course, but they also feed on just about any other flower that's available. Some of their favorites are in fact blue. Much of the time hummingbirds are not after nectar, but rather the insects attracted to the flowers.

A garden designed to keep hummingbirds around, rather

A broad-tailed hummingbird feeding its nestlings an insect treat.

than just cruising through occasionally, would have a succession of nectar-rich, brightly colored flowers, a feeder or two and some places to perch. Bill Fontenot employs a two part strategy to keep the tiny birds in his Louisiana garden—big, showy flowers like camellias to attract them, and smaller, nectar-rich species to keep them. This is a good strategy anywhere.

A young sapling or branch cut and "planted" among the flowers by the sugar-water feeder makes a great perch. Put one feeder in front, and another in back, in an effort to minimize territorial conflicts.

Across the extreme south, where the birds stay all year, some people go all-out to keep hummers in the garden. Tropical flowers like hibiscus get hauled in and out of garages and masses of perennials and annuals supplement a succession of shrubs and vines. It's almost as if the little birds are domesticating humans to care for them. But the north and west have hummers too—albeit only in the summer when enough flowers are blooming to support the tiny birds.

In Rockport, Texas, sight of an annual hummingbird festival, gardeners have learned to create several "rooms" in their gardens to cut down on feeder competition. Plants screen the views so birds at

one feeder won't feel compelled to chase after those at the next one. During the height of migration season, birds will "dive-bomb" anything red, including people with red clothing, hoping to find food. Gardeners farther north have reported birds fighting with them over red-flowered transplants they are trying to get in the ground.

Feeders left out during fall migration time in the northern areas will not keep birds from migrating south. Birds know when it is time and no sugar water will keep them. Those left behind are there for other reasons.

Hummingbirds are true jewels of the garden, busily buzzing about their business. The are not difficult to attract—if you create the right environment with flowers and feeders.

Hummingbird Feeders

The current advice on feeders is simple: fill them with a sugar-water solution made by mixing one part sugar to four parts boiling water, stirred until it dissolves. That's it. Keep unused solution in the refrigerator. Commercial food costs a lot more and is no better (and may be worse if it has other ingredients). For orioles, mix a weaker solution, one part sugar to six parts water. No coloring is

HUMMINGBIRD PLANTS

Here is a list of plants that will attract hummingbirds. Remember—a few specimens won't have as much attractive powers as a mass of blooms.

Acacia	*Acacia* spp.	Morning glory	*Ipomoea* spp.
Althaea	*Hibiscus syriacus*	Nasturtium	*Tropaeolum* spp.
Begonia	*Begonia* spp.	Oleander	*Nerium oleander*
Butterfly bush	*Buddleia* spp.	Citrus	*Citrus* spp.
Canna	*Canna* spp.	Passionflower	*Passiflora* spp.
Cardinal flower	*Lobelia cardinalis*	Petunia	*Petunia* spp.
Chinaberry	*Melia azederach*	Phlox	*Phlox* spp.
Clematis	*Clematis* spp.	Portulaca	*Portulaca* spp.
Columbine	*Aquilegia* spp.	Rose	*Rosa* spp.
Coral bells	*Heuchera* x *brizoides*	Sage	*Salvia* spp.
Eucalyptus	*Eucalyptus* spp.	Scarlet runner bean	*Phaseolus coccineus*
Four o'clock	*Mirabilis jalapa*		

Wild plants: East and Prairies

Fuchsia	*Fuchsia* spp.	Jewelweed	*Impatiens* spp.
Geranium	*Pelargonium* spp.	Painted cup	*Castilleja* spp.
Gladiolus	*Gladiolus* spp.	Morning glory	*Ipomoea* spp., *Convolvulus* spp.
Hibiscus	*Hibiscus* spp.		
Hollyhock	*Alcea* spp.		
Honeysuckle	*Lonicera* spp.		
Horse chestnut	*Aesculus* spp.		
Iris	*Iris* spp.		
Lantana	*Lantana* spp.		
Larkspur	*Consolida* spp.		
Lilac	*Syringa* spp.		
Lima bean	*Phaseolus lunatus*		
Mimosa	*Albizia* spp.		

Roses.

Impatiens.

Morning glory.

Coneflowers (foreground) and phlox (background).

Columbine.

Lilac.

needed for that either. The feeders usually have something red or orange to attract the birds.

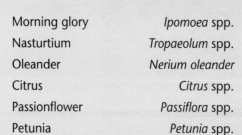

Use only plain sugar water without added color in hummingbird feeders.

Hang sugar-water feeders in the shade, especially in hot regions. Check frequently for mold, and change the solution and clean feeders at least several times a week, more often in hotter weather. Also, choose the largest feeders you can in hot areas since the liquid will evaporate quickly. Bee guards can help keep bees and wasps away, but they also sometimes bother the hummers. Another way to discourage bees and wasps, especially when tiny baby hummingbirds may be trying to feed, is to smear

something slippery like mineral oil on the outside of the feeder, keeping it away from the feeder opening. Wasps will have a hard time getting a foothold. Another strategy is to distract the pests with something else that's sweet and easy to lap up with their short tongues.

To clean feeders use warm water, adding a bit of vinegar if there is mold to clean up. If you need to do a more thorough job, scrub with a brush using a bit of dish soap and rinse thoroughly.

BUTTERFLIES

Daisies are reliable butterfly attractors.

Lilac.

When Margaret and John Dye settled in the country they decided to finally design a garden just they way they wanted it—to maximize their views of wildlife and minimize the work of mowing and other garden chores. From their kitchen table they can now watch birds all year and butterflies from earliest spring until late fall. They've counted 140 species. Field guides and binoculars are ready on the table when a newcomer shows up. The Dyes have a large lot to work with, but the principles they use to attract wildlife—especially butterflies—will work anywhere.

The year revolves around what's going on in the garden. Margaret has a succession of constant bloom, beginning with a patch of native wildlflowers in a shady area, soon followed by shrubs and perennials throughout the garden. Groundcovers, weeds, shrubs, perennials and annuals are all part of the display—59 species in all on a quick count in late spring. Her favorites include rudbeckia, daisy, phlox, monarda, lilacs, campanulas and salvias.

What makes the garden so attractive to butterflies is that it is a sheltered, sunny place with lots of nectar and larval food sources. Trees ring so that even on windy days there are spots that remain relatively still. The flowers are arranged cottage-garden style, with varying heights and colors. Mourning cloak butterflies that overwintered among the forest trees find nectar ready for them as soon as the snow melts. Red admirals seek out the early blooming lilacs. Masses of phlox are easily visible to later arrivals; New England asters take over in the fall and help the migrators stoke up.

Weeds are allowed to mix in, especially when they add flowers. The self-heal that is taking over the already-limited lawn in back was looking especially healthy, because they had been carefully mowing around it. Butterflies and hummingbirds, along with many native pollinators, love the clusters of little purple flowers.

Feeders and More

Use butterfly feeders only in relatively cool climates; in hot dry areas like the desert southwest, the fruit dries up quickly. Butterflies prefer flowers over fruit anyway.

Butterfly houses just don't seem to work. If there are shrubs, trees, grasses and brush piles available, butterflies will find plenty of places to roost and overwinter.

As for water, fill a shallow plant saucer with moist sand or gravel, cover with water, add a rock for basking and keep all contents moist. Set the water right in among your flowers. An area of moist soil works too.

It's hard to believe creatures as beautiful as butterflies would be drawn to manure and dead animals, but some are. A small pile of manure in the back of the flower bed will lure them. Pieces of overripe fruit will attract others. Try bananas, watermelons (the rind is fine), cantaloupe and grapes. When watering flowers, don't spray them because it washes away the nectar. Use soaker hoses instead.

Late blooming asters are important food for monarchs getting ready to fly south.

A gulf fritillary resting on impatiens.

Stone walls, stone stepping stones or rocks placed among the flowers are great basking places where you may be able to catch sight of a favorite butterfly at rest.

Nectar Plants

There are many lists of which flowers will attract butterflies. On some plants there is little disagreement that they are good for attracting butterflies. But for many others there are differing opinions. Some plants high on the list in one garden turn out to be duds in another. On the other hand, most garden flowers eventually show up on a list.

You can drive yourself crazy and try to plant exactly what your favorite butterfly may or may not want in your garden,

or you can adopt the shotgun approach. Plant a wide variety of flowers, focusing on constant bloom and including some of the known champions. Then watch what happens in your garden and in wild places nearby. When you find a new favorite, bring more of it in.

Common garden annuals that attract butterflies incude zinnias, tithonia, cosmos, marigold and impatiens (which wins hands-down). Southwest larval plants, including mesquite and desert penstemon are good in the arid climates. A plant the butterflies love, and is seldom mentioned, is *Salvia greggii*, or autumn sage. Its red flowers attract hummers, too.

Larval Plants

Butterfly and moth larvae are highly specific about what they eat. Sometimes it can be a single plant species, though more often they tend of focus on a family or genus. Monarchs have evolved eating milkweeds; they concentrate toxic substances produced by the plant to ward off predators. One taste of a monarch is enough to cure a bird forever, so that it even avoids butterflies that mimic the monarch, like the viceroy.

Swallowtails live on members of the parsley family, which includes dill and fennel. The gulf fritillary likes maypop and blue passionflower; the Eastern tiger swallowtail prefers the tulip tree. In fact, most good butterfly host plants are natives.

Mid-Atlantic

Milkweed	*Asclepias* spp.
New England aster	*Aster novae-angliae*
Butterfly bush	*Buddleia davidii*
Purple coneflower	*Echinacea purpurea*
Joe-Pye weed	*Eupatorium* spp.
Goldenrod	*Solidago* spp.
Mexican sunflower	*Tithonia rotundifolia*
Zinnia	*Zinnia elegans*

Southeast

Glossy abelia	*Abelia x grandiflora*
Butterfly weed	*Asclepias* spp.
Butterfly bush	
Lantana	*Lantana* spp.
Gayfeather	*Liatris* spp.
Summer phlox	*Phlox paniculata*
Mexican sunflower	
Verbena	*Verbena* spp.
Chaste tree	*Vitex agnus-castus*

Subtropical Florida

Golden dewdrop	*Duranta erecta*
Blanketflower	*Gaillardia* spp.
Firebush	*Hamelia patens*
Peregrina	*Jatropha integerrima*
Lantana	
Starflower	*Pentas lanceolata*
Scarlet sage	*Salvia splendens*
Mexican sunflower	

Common milkweed is one of the best native plants for butterfly gardens; it is difficult to transplant, so protect any that come up spontaneously.

Queen Anne's lace.

Dogbane.

BUTTERFLY PLANTS

Tiger swallowtail on centaurea (Mountain bluets).

Midwest

Dogbane	*Apocynum androsaemifolium*
Butterfly weed	
Asters	
New Jersey tea	*Ceanothus americanus*
Purple coneflower	
Gayfeather	
Bee balm	*Monarda* spp.
Catnip	*Nepeta cataria*
Goldenrod	
Marigold	*Tagetes* spp.

Rocky Mountains/Great Plains

Butterfly weed	
Butterfly bush	
Red valerian	*Centranthus ruber*
Leadwort	*Plumbago auriculata*
Wallflower	*Cheiranthus cheiri*
Gayfeather	
Garden phlox	
Pincushion flower	*Scabiosa* spp.
Verbena	

Southwest

Wild hyssop	*Agastache* spp.
Milkweed	
Desert willow	*Chilopsis linearis*
Rabbitbrush	*Chrysothamnus nauseosus*
Ocotillo	*Fouquieria splendens*
Lantana	

Purple aster	*Machaeranthera bigelovii*
Cherry sage	*Salvia coccinea*
Verbena	

Southern Coastal California

Milkweed	
Coastal buckwheat	*Eriogonum fasciculatum*
Impatiens	*Impatiens wallerana*
Lantana	
Deerweed	*Lotus scoparius*
Monkey flower	*Mimulus* spp.
Rosemary	*Rosmarinus officinalis*
Goldenrod	
Marigold	
Zinnia	

Pacific Northwest

Yarrow	*Achillea* spp.
Anise hyssop	*Agastache foeniculum*
Butterfly bush	
Red valerian	
Pinks	*Dianthus* spp.
Joe-Pye weed	
Sunflower	*Helianthus* spp.
Bee balm	
Phlox	
Stonecrop	*Sedum* spp.

Southeast

Azalea	*Rhododendron* spp.
Butterfly bush	*Glossy abelia*
Lantana	
Cosmos	*Cosmos* spp.
Heliotrope	*Heliotropium arborescens*
Impatiens	
Mexican sunflower	
Moss verbena	*Verbena tenuisecta*
Zinnia	

Achillea (yellow).

Fritillary on coneflower.

Sunflower.

Butterfly weed attracts many butterflies.

◀ CHAPTER 7 ▶

WHEN WILDLIFE IS A PROBLEM

Wildlife in the garden is sometimes a mixed blessing. Eventually, some bird, animal or insect oversteps the boundaries of acceptable behavior and causes tension. The most important advice for gardeners is to cultivate patience, examine carefully what has happened, then consider the options for stemming the problem. As one gardener said to me, "Sure, some animals can be irritating, but at times so are the people we love." You learn to live and let live.

Cute as they can be, raccoons are not always popular among gardeners.

A few chipmunks are fun to have around, but when their population explodes you may have to take steps to protect bulbs.

Take chipmunks. They're charming, furry little creatures that scamper about and stuff their cute little cheek pouches with seeds or nuts, right? Not to everyone. One year the Parrens' garden was overrun with chipmunks.

The little rodents were everywhere, running about all day making little highways leading to and from the spillover seed under the bird feeder, and being bold enough to sit on one of the children's feet. That spring, the garden's tulips never came up; the lilies were missing too, also devoured by the hungry chipmunk hordes.

The family's reaction varied. Lauren, the main gardener who loves her perennial borders, was less than thrilled and had fantasies of what she'd like to do to the little marauders (possibly with the help of dogs and cats).

When you invite wildlife into your garden, be prepared for some compromises. To them, this is all potential food or shelter.

Keeping squirrels out of birdfeeders is difficult at best, but counterbalanced birdfeeders that shut under their weight seem to work—at least for a while.

Steve, wildlife biologist to the core, noted the increase with interest and, taking the long view, figured that natural predators or disease would eventually take care of the problem. (He also brought home some new perennials to compensate Lauren for "his" chipmunks' destructive behavior.) The girls continued to be delighted with the little creatures and secretly supplied them with seeds when their parents weren't looking.

A few weeks later, humor and patience had prevailed. There was still some muttering about chipmunks and hopes for large, hungry snakes, but Lauren had resolved to plant more daffodils the next fall, since chipmunks don't touch them. "What are you going to do?" she said, laughing. With the great variety of flowers in that garden, it still looked spectacular all season.

The lesson is that humans, their gardens and wildlife can coexist if we can flex our goals and standards just a little bit.

When Co-existing Doesn't Work

Unfortunately, not all situations with wildlife are easy to resolve. There are times when the boundaries crossed are more serious. Few people, no matter how much they love wildlife, want them living in the house, where damage can be done. Sometimes the plants wildlife harms matter enough to warrant some drastic action. And there are times when wild animals pose a physical danger to people.

Although it is upsetting to lose a prized plant or find holes in the yard, animals are not doing this out of spite or to upset humans—they are merely going about their business of finding food and shelter in a world increasingly inhospitable to them. Unfortunately, with all the gadgets, chemical remedies and exterminators available to deal with unexpected intruders, much violence and unnecessary destruction take place. What's more, too often people blame the wrong culprit or misunderstand the reason for the intrusion and overreact. This is entirely contrary to the spirit of wildlife gardening, which strives always to see the garden as a whole, and as part of a larger system.

The following discussion is divided into sections, based on the most commonly enountered wildlife troublemakers: insects; squirrels at birdfeeders; bird and mammal damage to crops; digging and burrowing pests; intruders in the house; and some potentially problematic visitors that could endanger pets or humans.

Physical barriers are by far the safest way to keep animals away, so the main focus is on those. These barriers harm nobody and leave no residues to affect other animals. Labels on commercial products designed to keep deer or rabbits away, for example, say things like "toxic to aquatic species, keep away from water," or "causes irreversible damage to eyes if contacted." These can harm a lot more than the pest you're targeting. Repellents like hot pepper and garlic sprays, coyote urine, human hair or containers of ammonia left to perfume the air may well discourage some pests some of the time.

INSECTS

Most insects in gardens do little or no damage and are best kept in balance by other creatures that eat them.

Spray as a Last Resort

Once when I was doing research on live oaks in Louisiana, a member of a tree care crew described to me how he usually recommended that people regularly spray their trees thoroughly. "You wouldn't believe how many insects live up there," he told me. This attitude is fairly widespread. All those insects are just assumed to be a problem, when in fact they are an essential part of the ecosystem.

But some insects do cause problems, especially when they have a population explosion. That's when the insecticides come out. But even a "natural" spray, unless it is incredibly specific, will kill other insects, including beneficial ones such as pollinators and the caterpillars of the very butterflies we want to attract to the garden. Detailed insect control is beyond the scope of this book, but the main approach already described— don't panic, see what natural

predators will do given a little time—is the best place to start and may lead to new insights about the garden ecosystem. If you must control insects, use the least toxic method you can find. Hand-pick beetles or caterpillars, or spray with a water hose—one of the soap sprays or a specifically targeted control.

Use a Physical Barrier

Physical barriers are a simple way to exclude some of the consistent problems in the vegetable garden, like the introduced white cabbage butterfly. Lightweight fabric row covers, stretched directly over crops or held above them with hoops, will keep many flying pests from landing and depositing eggs. Yet a good population of birds is one of best ways to limit insect damage, and some animals labeled pests, like opossums, love to eat snails.

Entrap Them

"Trap crops" are a way of concentrating damage on a few plants to protect others. In Barbara Nardozzi's garden, evening primroses are often infested, sparing other flowers. One year caterpillars devoured the swamp milkweed, as they had the year before. She wasn't concerned, and was excited to know the next generation of butterflies would be coming along soon. The plants had bloomed, and had apparently not suf-

fered too much from the previous season's munching.

The hop vine is always chewed terribly during the first month or two of growth. Then it begins to produce fine healthy leaves. Insect cycles and plant cycles often have such relationships, allowing each to get what it needs to survive. It is that the gardeners want every plant perfect that is more often the problem.

Look Ahead

Before using any chemical product, "natural" or not, read all labels and consider what else might be affected by what you do. Any change affects the whole system in some way, often in ways you may not be able to predict. Unless the situation is dangerous or simply intolerable, wait. Often slight imbalances will right themselves if you can tolerate damage in the short term.

Lightweight row covers are good ways to exclude flying or hopping insects coming to lay eggs or chew on tender seedlings.

SQUIRRELS AT BIRDFEEDERS

Masters of Trickery

Whole books have been written about how to deal with squirrels. It's almost as if this species was put on earth to remind humans that no matter how clever we believe ourselves to be, we are not in charge.

It is also instructive to remember that the main problem with tree squirrels centers around our own invention—the birdfeeder.

One year, I found myself constantly leaping at the kitchen window and yelling to scare the squirrels off the feeder. Then, as they jumped to safety, they'd spill so much seed on the ground they could feed there uninterrupted for a long time. Finally it came to me—stop putting seed in the feeder. What a relief. No squirrels, no yelling and plenty of birds in the shrubs all around the house and at the feeder next door.

Most gardeners would not begrudge the shy nocturnal flying squirrel a few bird seeds in midwinter.

Baffles on poles below bird feeders are one way to discourage squirrels and raccoons. Make sure they are wide and deep enough to keep the animals from reaching around them.

If squirrels only knew how much time and money people have invested in keeping them out of bird feeders, they'd probably laugh. On the other hand, plenty of gardeners are highly amused at squirrels methodically outwitting each ploy. One gardener told me her daughter had tried hot pepper mixed with bird seed only to find the squirrels just loved it. She then tried smearing the feeder pole with vaseline and found this was better than watching funniest home videos. She'd get her tea to sit and watch the largest of their squirrel troop as he leaped six feet in the air and slid all the way down. After about 50 leaps, he wore the vaseline off and could get back up to eat. The next time she smeared the pole, he knew just what to do.

Physical Barriers

The best physical barrier for squirrels and other climbing mammals is a large, cone-shaped metal guard, wide enough that they cannot reach around it (see photo). Placed around a pole that is far enough away from roofs and trees so that they cannot leap to the feeder on top, this rig really works. These cones are also good for protecting nesting boxes.

Another feeder protection program that works is a wire strung between two trees, holding a dome-type plastic feeder. Keeping the squirrels at bay are four large plastic soda bottles strung end to end on each side of the feeder. The squirrels can't get a grip on them.

Distract Them

Another option is to feed the squirrels something they really like—corn—at another location. Some generous gardeners feed squirrels away from the bird feeder. You can also distract them by scattering mixed nuts and seeds on a low platform; this will also attract juncos, cardinals and other ground-feeding birds.

DAMAGE TO PLANTS AND GARDENS

Browsing Mammals

Vegetarian animals are the worst offenders in vegetable and ornamental gardens. In the wild, browsing can actually stimulate growth of plants, but yews pruned by deer have a ragged look that understandably offends gardeners. And while birds might be efficient distributers of fruit tree seeds, most of us would prefer to harvest cherries or apples ourselves.

Deer

Repellents of all kinds are good for keeping deer away and human hair is one of the best. A friend in the midwest, desperate to protect yew plants right by the house, heard from a friend that human hair would deter deer. She brought a whole bag of hair home from the hairdresser. About March, when the deer were once again beginning to chow down on the yews, she decided it was time to try the hair. Not sure exactly how to go about this, she walked around with the bag held at arm's length, dumping it on the yews. The result was weird-looking, especially the extra long strands of grey draped here and there, but the deer stayed away.

Later, the deer began to munch on new tulip leaves, threatening to ruin the flower borders. Out came the hair again, spread among the bulbs, and it again discouraged the deer. The tulips managed to send up perfectly fine blooms among flat-topped leaves. Later that season, as the deer moved on to an old apple tree in the yard, she stuffed more hair among the crotches and managed once more to discourage them. One neat way to distribute human hair is to stuff it into old pantyhose (which let the scent escape), then place the hose strategically.

Hair, coyote urine, rotten eggs and other substances emit smells that will deter some deer in some situations. None of them is foolproof, but they are relatively innocuous deterrents worth trying.

Deer-resistant plantings are another approach. Long lists have been compiled, for different regions, of plants deer like and don't like. The only trouble is when gardeners and researchers started comparing notes, they found amazing disagreements—not only between different areas, but in different years. Deer develop certain tastes, so that there is little telling what an individual animal or herd is likely to go for at any time.

Is there a foolproof solution? That depends on the goal. If you want to absolutely

Two deer repellents that use scents: On top of the pole are rags soaked in a commercial formula, then covered with a pail. Hanging at right are panty hose stuffed with human hair.

Black-tailed deer browsing in a northwest meadow.

Wire fencing arched over vulnerable young plants protects them from hungry deer.

Rabbits, like deer, love succulent green growth, and in winter will nibble on bark and twigs.

Havahart traps are a humane way to remove troublesome creatures, such as racoons, squirrels and woodchucks, from your yard.

prevent deer damage on your property, a tall fence, at least 8 feet high all around, can accomplish that. A more economical solution is to group the plants you care about most, and that deer also seem to love, and fence them in back of the house or in a place deer would feel exposed. Of course, the more people fence their yards, the higher the pressure on remaining open ones, and fences keep out other creatures, as well.

Deer prefer young succulent growth. Covering seedlings and young woody plants with netting can protect them until they mature enough that deer will leave them alone, or at least not destroy them entirely. Some fine black netting is hardly visible, and much less expensive than fencing.

Rabbits

Rabbits also love succulent new growth like that of young garden seedlings. In winter, they sometimes strip away tree bark to get at the soft layers below, and will nibble at twigs and buds. A 3-foot tall chicken wire fence (1 inch mesh or the rabbits will slip through), buried one foot in the ground, will keep bunnies out of the garden. Gates with sills on the bottom prevent rabbits from burrowing underneath. Once the plants are mature, the fence may not be necessary. A planting of clover and alfalfa away from the garden might keep rabbits away from the vegetables, too.

To protect trees and shrubs in winter, wrap the trunks with wire mesh that extends 2 feet above snow line and 4 inches below ground.

Predators will manage rabbits efficiently, too. Foxes and owls can take care of a lot of rabbit problems quickly.

Woodchucks

These persistent animals can drive gardeners to distraction, quickly decimating a vegetable garden. Woodchucks don't travel far from their burrows in search of food. One line of defense is a scarecrow. Fencing that extends 3 feet high, and 1 to 2 feet underground, may be a better solution. Woodchucks also gnaw on trees and wood to wear down winter growth of teeth and sharpen claws; if 'chucks are regulars in your garden, barriers around tree trunks may also be a good idea.

Raccoons and Corn

If you grow corn, and there are raccoons in your area, you're in for a battle. Raccoons have an uncanny sense for when corn is almost ripe and inevitably get to it just before people harvest the crop. This isn't too surprising—raccoons are out there every night on their regular rounds, and know the signs of ripeness. They start working the crop the minute it is palatable to them. There are often plenty of growers and farmers' markets at which to buy corn, and it simply isn't worth the space and time spent putting up fencing.

If you want to win, though, electric fencing (put up early) is the best deterrent. Fortunately there are lightweight, relatively inexpensive poles and generators now available, with easily adjusted strands. The best strand spacing for raccoons is one close to the ground, about 2 inches, with the second at 8 inches and the third 15 inches from the ground. This fence should also keep out rabbits.

Tree Guards

Animals damage tree trunks when they chew away outer bark to get at the tender layers within, especially in winter when food is scarce. Buck deer also like to polish their antlers on young tree trunks in early fall. Commercial

Woodchucks are phenomenal diggers who tend not to travel far from home.

Wire mesh wrapped around tree trunks will discourage gnawing creatures looking for food, especially in winter. For better protection, bury the lower part an inch or 2 into the ground.

tree wraps of various kinds are available to prevent this type of damage. For rabbits, wrap an area that extends above the snow line in winter. For voles, which travel below snow line, bury the wrap 6 to 8 inches deep, using 1/4- inch mesh.

Sheet metal wrapped around the tree can keep squirrels and opossums from harvesting nuts and fruit, but only if there is no other way to get up into the tree. Squirrels can easily jump 5 to 6 feet into the air, so get the metal up above your head. They can jump much farther than that from neighboring trees or roofs.

Birds

In England, I remember being amazed the first time I saw fruit cages, whole sections of gardens enclosed with sturdy mesh to keep cherries, currants and gooseberries safe from voracious birds. These cages come in a range of sizes and designs, with doors to admit the gardener. American gardeners have adopted this idea. In Tucson, Arizona, I've seen the same basic technique used to protect a whole vegetable garden of raised beds. In that dry climate, anything as green and lush as that garden was a magnet for just about any animal interested in food or water.

Check out garden supply catalogs to locate these cages, or rig your own version with poles and chickenwire or netting. Within that protection, you can plant any crops or flowers you do not want to share.

A less expensive approach is to use netting on single trees. The net need only be on the tree when fruits are ripening (though check early because some birds start eating when the fruit is still green). Netting for this purpose, in different sizes for trees or shrubs, is available from many mail-order nursery catalogs. For best results, gather the netting tightly around the trunk, or hold it down with weights around the edge.

Seedlings in the vegetable garden are often under attack from birds and insects. Row covers and individual covers can keep down damage there. Lightweight fabrics, or netting stretched over hoops, allow enough light to pass through.

Opossums generally don't do much damage around homes and may help by eating insects and other invertebrates.

RABIES

Fear about rabies is generally out of proportion to the problem the disease truly presents. But it's worth some thought.

Bats are often blamed but less than one-half of one percent of bats ever get rabies, a rate similar to that of other animals like racoons and dogs. Skunks are often thought of as carriers of rabies as well.

The difference is that even if bats are infected, they don't become aggressive as do dogs or raccoons and they seldom transmit the disease except to other bats. Plus, infected individuals die quickly, so they seldom have outbreaks as do other species.

The best defense against rabies is to avoid animals that are unusually friendly or unafraid of humans, and to call local authorities if you see any that are walking in circles, approaching pets, acting strange or not being afraid of humans. Be sure to keep your pets vaccinated at all times.

A sturdy wooden frame covered with black plastic netting will keep birds out of berry plantings; the English have long used such cages in their gardens.

DIGGING AND BURROWING PESTS

Star-nosed moles seldom see daylight. Their diet includes soil grubs and other underground invertebrates.

Moles make shallow surface tunnels in lawn that can collapse or get torn by mower blades.

Identify the Culprit

Identifying the source of digging and burrowing problems is the first challenge, since so many of these creatures are nocturnal.

Squirrels sometimes feel compelled to dig in flower boxes. No doubt they have their reasons...possibly to get at flavorful-smelling roots, or maybe just because they like to dig.

Armadillos and skunks that dig in the lawn or garden are looking for grubs and probably not interested in your plants. For chipmunks and squirrels, place coarse wire mesh right on the planting bed; this also works in window boxes that sometimes fascinate squirrels. After planting, put chicken wire or finer mesh over the soil and cover it with a layer of mulch.

Pocket gophers are tough to repel with fencing. For small areas, 1/2-inch or 1/4-inch hardware cloth, buried 18 to 20 inches deep, helps also keep ground damp, as dampness isn't good for burrowing. Get rid of weeds and groundcover to cut down on food (contrary to most of the rest of the directions in this book).

Gophers bite off plants from underneath, causing damage. These vegetarians seem to love grasses and alfalfa. Gophers actually aerate soil with their constant tunneling. Gophers have separate cone shaped mounds at their tunnel entrances. An old stand-by defense is to keep tunnel entrances plugged when gophers are inside. You can also flood tunnels to drive gophers out.

Fighting Moles

Moles can cause great problems with their destructive, tunneling habits. Here is a way to foil these underground pests.

To protect flower beds from moles, dig up about 6 inches of soil and make a wavy base with chicken wire. Then fill back in with soil. This can foil moles for up to five years—until the chicken wire disintegrates. The only problem is you can't till the soil without re-doing the net protector each year. Instead, clip the old crop and wait a week or so to let the roots decompose then plant right in among them. If moles are out in your yard, tunneling through and destroying your grass, an exterminator may be your best bet. Insist on physical, not chemical, means of taking care of the problem.

Armadillos, which constantly dig up ground in search of food, are one of the few animals that eat fire ants.

INTRUDERS IN THE HOUSE

Animals come into houses to find shelter and food. The best way to keep them out is to shut pet doors at night. Skunks, racoons and opossums can easily find their way into houses in search of food (often lured by pet food left out and smelling perfectly delicious) and cause all kinds of trouble. If you must have a pet door, set it so it allows your dog or cat to go out, but not to come in.

Some animals may come in to find a den site, or a place to hibernate. Skunks love it under porches. Bats, racoons and squirrels find attics a fine substitute for caves and hollow trees. These visitors' goals are not to threaten people or harm the house, although often they do cause damage.

As with the garden, the best defense is to physically close off access to the where you don't want the intruders. That means checking all openings to the outside and covering them with screens or solid material. In some cases it also means covering telephone wires or removing branches that allow animals to reach the roof easily. The humane approach is to do this when there are no babies that might be abandoned inside—not only is that cruel, but it will make the whole proceeding more difficult (and potentially smelly).

If you have animals living in your house and are unsure how to proceed, contact local wildlife organizations for advice. Exterminators who use chemical substances of any kind probably cause more harm to you and your family than the animals would. Unless entrances to the house are blocked, other pests will show up again eventually.

Occasionally animals might stray into a house, having flown or crawled inside in search of food or to find cover. They generally want to get out as much as you want them out, and they are scared. The best policy is to leave doors and windows open and go away. Otherwise harmless creatures such as skunks, racoons and squirrels, when cornered, will bite to defend themselves.

Rosalind Creasy told me a skunk story. A skunk lived under their bedroom in Los Altos for a while, raising a family. Not only was there a constant smell, but each night the skunks would decide to do some home improvements just as Ros and her husband were trying to go to sleep. Finally the home-

DANGER: SNAKES

You have a better chance of drowning or being killed by lightning than you do of dying from a snakebite. But it's still worth a few precautionary measures to avoid confrontations with rattlesnakes, cottonmouths, copperheads and coral snakes— our country's poisonous snakes.

Don't have high grass or brush piles near your house. Never put your hands or feet where you can't see them—such as under boards or rocks or tree limbs. Look where you're walking. Wear shoes at all times.

And don't panic (that's easy to say) when you see a snake. Stop, don't make any aggressive moves and back off slowly but surely to get out of its striking range. Try to identify the snake, but don't touch it or catch it.

If you do happen to get bit and the snake is poisonous, the best treatment is to stay calm and get to an emergency room as quickly as possible. Having someone drive you is best. Cutting the wound and sucking the venom out has been proven to be an old wive's tale. Your best care is under the supervision of a physician.

Poisonous snakes are a problem few gardeners will ever have to worry about. Most of the snakes that visit your yard will cause no harm to you, and in fact will be beneficial in the pest control services they provide.

Get to know the few poisonous snakes, like the rattlesnake, so that you can stop worrying about the many beneficial species that might wander into the garden sometime.

owners had had enough. One day Robert watched the skunks all leave, then boarded and bricked the opening shut. For several weeks they had to listen to the skunks clawing at the barrier trying to get back in, before giving up.

Boards, bricks, cement, steel wool around pipes...all these keep pests out.

Bats

Bats can come into houses through open doors and windows, loose fitting screens, chimneys and any hole more than $1/2$-inch in diameter. They may fly in after insects, then be unable to find their way out. Or they may stray from roost sites in the attic and get into the house proper.

Often it is young bats that become lost in a house; all they want is to get out. One way to catch a scared bat is to put an empty paper-towel tube, one end sealed, next to the bat as it clings to a wall or other surface. It will crawl in to hide and you cover up the other end of the tube and take the bat outside.

A few bats in the attic pose no threat to humans, but one of the species that form large colonies can be a potential health problem. To evict them, observe the same basic approach as with other animals. Wait until the young are independent, generally by midsummer. Cover all entrance holes with netting at night, placed so that bats can find their way out, but not back in.

Keep doors securely shut and make pet doors one way, going out, to prevent racoons or possums from ransacking the house for food.

CHAPTER 8

ENJOYING YOUR BACKYARD HABITAT AND BEYOND

The real magic in wildlife gardening is the transformation of gardeners. It doesn't happen by accident. Creating a garden that is inviting to wildlife is one step—having certain plants arranged to make wildlife feel at home, adding food and water sources, avoiding things that could harm them.

But just as important is to create places and times where people can get to know who's out there. That's what really changes attitudes. When gardeners switch their gardening approach from one of control to one of stewardship and cooperation, they find themselves spending a lot of time watching the animals that come, tracking the annual cycles and noting changes through the years.

Benches and swings in the garden, a tree house and quiet woodland paths all give people chances to observe the life around them. It is living in relationship to other creatures that so enriches the lives of wildlife gardeners and often inspires them to carry their convictions beyond their own yards.

Working together in your wildlife garden can be an enjoyable and rewarding experience.

LEARNING TO SEE

Learn to look closely into brush piles, under rocks, behind trees. A well camouflaged song sparrow nest becomes a brood of hungry chicks, and if you are patient, you will see the young birds take off on their first flight.

The Art of Observing

Learning to observe is as much an art as is the making of the garden. It takes time. Animals don't automatically show up in response to certain plants, nor do they pose conveniently whenever we're moved to glance at the garden. In a culture that rushes about as frantically as most of us do, it is distinctly counter-cultural to sit quietly waiting to see a butterfly or moth, to listen expectantly for the song of a rare bird at dawn or dusk, to crouch in the shrubbery hoping for a glimpse of tree

Only careful looking will reveal a quiet tree frog resting on a leaf.

frogs. And yet this simple kind of being in the garden—receptive, paying attention to details—is a most restorative and satisfying activity.

Timing it Right

Timing is crucial. Early morning is for the birds, and perhaps some of the shy mammals that are active mostly at night. The combination of sounds, early morning light and the quick views of color and movement are a great way to start the day, either sitting quietly outside or drifting slowly through the garden. Late afternoon the birds go through another period of singing and feeding; some species are active all day.

For late sleepers, butterflies may be a better focus. They like the heat of midday, and are most active when it's sunny. There is no predicting exactly when and where you will see them. But just resting your eyes on colorful flower beds is a pleasure, and after a while you begin to detect the butterflies' small movements out of the corner of your eye, and learn to approach them carefully. Some will skip right by, but eventually you may be

rewarded with the breathtaking view of a painted lady, lazily opening and closing its spectacular wings as it pokes its proboscis into one after another of the florets on a zinnia.

Enjoy the Details

Butterfly watching might slow you down enough so that the next smaller creatures, the many pollinators, catch your attention. Large gaudy flowers attract them; but so do the smaller fragrant blooms. Flowers are just alive with all kinds of insects and others hoping for meal.

Stop to examine a milkweed some day and you'll be astounded at the variety of life there. Some unlucky insects get caught by their hind legs on the flowers. Spiders lurk ready to

Midday is a good time to look for butterflies in a sun-filled meadow.

Tiny lizards flit about bright blossoms in southern gardens.

ambush other visitors. Eggs and larvae dot the leaves. Sometimes a monarch caterpillar will be munching or getting ready for its great transformation.

A hand lens is an inexpensive tool that provides an instant window into this miniature world, showing up startling details and often great, unexpected beauty.

Lizards are among the few creatures likely to be active during a hot day in the desert. Elsewhere, too, they will dart about rapidly after their prey, dashing across garden paths if startled.

Night Performances

Later, as the sun goes down, small ground-dwelling mammals will come out to look for seeds and insects. Evening is also when raccoons and opossums come out to prowl for food, deer and rabbits venture forth from hiding, and bats begin their evening pest patrol.

Sounds are important at night, and are often the only clue about who's out there. Toads and frogs come out of their damp hiding places to hunt, starting their daily chorus by any pond nearby. Owls hoot. In the garden, moths attend night-blooming flowers. Wherever bright lights shine, many species of moths, along with other insects, collect.

Know Their Routines

Many animals have regular routines; once you note them, you can be on the lookout. Studies that trace the nightly travels of individual raccoons show they usually cover the same ground each night on their rounds. A chipmunk that shared a porch and stone wall with me used to come out to the same spot each day to munch on its latest find, and another was almost always on a tree stump I passed on my afternoon walk.

Birds that know they are safe and can rely on food and water sources often show up in gardens at the same time each day.

Arrange bird baths, flower beds, feeders and other wildlife habitat attractants so that they are easily visible from strategic spots in your house. That way, the wildlife can become a part of your daily routine—watching the goldfinches take their morning bath as you eat breakfast, or observing butterflies as you do dishes at the sink window.

Sit Still

Sitting still is a good technique to work on. That alone is often enough to get close looks at usually shy animals, birds and insects.

When I lived in Louisiana, I used to sit for hours reading in the shade of a huge pecan tree in my backyard, trying to stay cool when the heat was oppressive in summer. Squirrels, lizards and birds got so used to my being there day after day, hardly moving, that they would come quite close as they searched the ground for food.

Animals perceive so differently from the way we do, relying far more on scent and movement than we to distinguish other animals or spot potential danger. Sudden movements scare them, as do figures that loom above them. Some can detect small eye movements and others have 360 degree vision, so it's no wonder it's often hard to sneak up on them.

Use Field Guides

Field guides are essential if you want to correctly identify species in the garden. Knowing the names of all your visitors is fun, and leads you to another level of appreciation. Although the number of species in a field guide can seem overwhelming

To fully appreciate visitors to your bird bath, put it where you can see it easily.

at first, after a while it gets more and more interesting (see appendix for some suggestions).

Insects will begin to sort themselves into groups. You will notice an unusual butterfly when it shows up. For some groups, like frogs and toads, it takes a little longer to learn the different markings and shapes of species. It helps me to compare notes with a friend.

Use Optics

One of best investments for wildlife watching is a pair of binoculars. They open up a whole new world, and enable identification of many more species. A magnification of 7x or 8x is about right for backyard viewing. To choose a pair, look through different kinds and see what feels comfortable and lets light in. For backyard birdwatching, the larger models are fine. For hiking I like a smaller pair.

Binoculars help with closer targets, too, especially those elu-sive butterflies that flit about restlessly and rush off if you get anywhere near them. Choose binoculars with a close focus option that allows you to zero in on nearby objects as well as distant ones.

Blinds

Hunters have long used blinds to remain invisible to their prey, a technique also adopted by wildlife watchers. Houses are good blinds themselves; birds get used to coming right up to windows to feed. Cars also work well. Birdwatchers know they can often get quite close to their quarry by just pulling the car over to the side of the road and watching from within. A single human figure outside the car would be much scarier.

In the garden, a gazebo or a seat partially screened by shrubs can act as a blind. A section of fencing, or a special structure made by nailing a series of boards to uprights with one removed at eye height works too, especially for viewing a pond or feeding station. The idea is to keep as much of your body hidden as possible, and to screen any sign of movement.

Quietly Observe

Regular visits, and lots of sitting quietly, are the best way to accustom animals to your presence. Avoid sudden movements, focusing on slowly changing position if necessary, instead of thrusting an arm or leg or shaking your head. Make sure your blind or observation spot is comfortable. I used to take my children to an Audubon center with a blind that overlooked a beaver pond. A few times we managed to see the beavers, but what I remember most is how uncomfortable it was in there. Ideally you should be able to sit relaxed,

Binoculars are invaluable in helping you see birds, butterflies and other visitors to the garden without frightening them away.

Contemplative traditions have much to teach the gardener who wants to encounter wildlife in the backyard.

back supported, neck not straining.

Learn From Kids

Children are often masters of observation, patiently watching the work of ants and other low-to-the ground wildlife. They'll often notice details of backyard wildife that adults miss.

It was Elena, Barbara and Charlie Nardozzi's daughter, who found and befriended a grey tree frog that lives on their back porch. She is also fond of the small garter snake that suns itself on the front stoop. In fact, most children I've met are far more interested in animals than in plants. The Parrens' daughters were appalled when a visiting boy suggested chasing the chipmunks for fun and explained to him that they did not treat animals that way in their yard.

Collecting animals for observation is a fine activity to encourage, as long as it does not harm the animals or bring children in contact with potential danger. The best approach is to keep the animals only briefly, then release them into the wild again. A bug box made with a screen on one end is perfect for watching an insect for a while then releasing it unharmed. Bringing in a butterfly chrysalis to watch the transformation into adult is a great family activity. I know one gardener who regularly has at least 30 of these jars in her house.

Stores and catalogs have all kinds of books and resources for wildlife activities. Although intended for children, there is no reason adults can't use them too. Keeping reference books on hand can help with quick identifications, and in some cases it can lead to a lifetime interest in animal studies. Elena already has quite a library of books on animals from all over the world, and another young boy I know will sit, enraptured, reading a guide to snakes.

Hand lenses, noted earlier, are a surprisingly powerful tool that opens up another level of wildlife watching for kids. Seeing the details of flowers, scales of a butterfly wing or eye of a fly are all instructive nature lessons.

Keep a Diary

Keeping a garden diary is a great activity for a family or individual. Barbara Nardozzi has been doing this for years. She tracks blooming and fruiting times of plants. She also notes when birds return from the south. For instance, each year an osprey shows up on Earth Day, fishes in the pond for a few days, then moves on.

The diary has helped her see patterns she might otherwise not note. She can look up the date that the chipmunks usually emerge from their winter sleep, or recall the time her son spotted a fox by the pond. The family's rhythms of life are becoming more closely tied to those of the world in her garden.

Garden records help build a history of your own garden. In it you can record which plants the butterflies like best, where you saw the hummingbird most often, which birds harvest the viburnum or mahonia berries. Note which shrubs are in fruit when in your garden, in other gardens, along the roadside and at nature centers; this will help you fill in gaps in your own plantings. Writing things down can change what you see. It focuses attention and increases your awareness of details that might otherwise slip by unnoticed. The goal is not to record only the exotic and unusual, but to appreciate the ordinary. Over time, such records become your story as well as the story of your garden.

Surround a gazebo with plants and you have a great blind for watching wildlife unobserved.

BEYOND THE GARDEN

Get Involved

The community of wildlife gardeners is growing rapidly, making connections among individuals and among other groups that have been around for years. Some naturalists and wildlife specialists concerned over habitat destruction are working to transform whole communities into places friendly to wildlife. Many leaders in this area are just people like you and me who started out by simply caring. Non-gardeners have become gardeners, realizing that horticultural skill is not the only measure of garden success, and that their own instincts and observations can help them create habitats for themselves and wildlife.

For example, Lorrie Otto started innocently enough. She was upset about a neighboring piece of land in her suburb that got drained and developed, so that there were no longer wild places for children to play. Then she got interested in prairie plants, and started putting them in her back yard. Soon she was known as the "wildflower lady" who gave tours of her garden to local brownie troops and others. Then she began to spend time with some other gardeners interested in native plants. The group became known as "The Wild Ones."

They began to meet regularly and have speakers, which in turn brought new members. By the early 1990s, they had 150 members in the north Milwaukee area. Since then, the group has grown quickly. Now there are more than 2000 members, with 12 chapters. Although most are still in the midwest, the group has gone national, with members from as far away as Manitoba, Florida and New York. Run entirely by volunteers, the organization publishes a journal and newsletter and has an annual meeting in the Milwaukee area.

One of their most effective strategies is an annual tour of yards landscaped with native plants. Lorrie started these tours years ago, and they've become a major fundraiser for the local Audubon Society chapter. Tour participants visit beautiful yards in Milwaukee suburbs, finishing up at Lorrie's own yard.

Wandering in the soothing shade of native woodland species or strolling along paths where tall prairie flowers bloom at eye-level, gardeners can see first-hand the possibilities of regionally appropriate gardens.

Rescue digs are another of their projects. Wild Ones members cultivate good relationships with developers, so that when some piece of land is about to be altered, they can go and dig up trees, grasses or any other plants for replanting in gardens. Although their first focus was on the plantings, the natural result has been that native wildlife follows.

Brett Rapraport, president of the group, is an attorney who started out defending gardeners who had run-ins with weed laws when they put in natural landscapes; now he has a prairie patch at his own home and speaks at national meetings about the topic.

Whether it's a teak bench, a simple slab of wood or a flat rock, the wildlife garden needs places to stop and look, listen, smell and feel.

Ecological Gardening

One of the best known writers on the topic of ecological gardening is Sara Stein. She started restoring a piece of land in New York and has now written two books about her own experiences putting in a meadow, redoing a pond to make it more attractive to wildlife, and discovering native plants and animals throughout the year. When she gave a workshop on her approach once, the participants just refused to leave until they had formed a group that would meet regularly. They called themselves "The Naturals" and would regularly visit each other's gardens to learn and suggest solutions and often help with plantings.

Form Your Own Group

Finding other like-minded gardeners is probably the best way to continue learning about wildlife gardening in your own region. Together you can work on ways to adapt the basic techniques and find local models to solve challenges. It isn't always obvious where to find the necessary information, since we are dealing with topics usually considered separate—native plants, wildlife habitat, vegetable gardening, water gardening ornamentals, watering, ecology, insect life cycles, lawn care, prairie restoration, pruning…the list goes on. A bit of discussion with others can be extremely helpful. Consulting experts within these many areas is also helpful.

Talk to the Experts

A whole cadre of specialists is slowly developing, generally specializing in one region or type of habitat. Bill Fontenot in Louisiana regularly gives workshops and lectures with standing room only; he's talked to groups throughout the southeast. Regional specialization is crucial, since there are so many different situations in different ecoregions.

To Coexist

There are opportunities for making major changes that could benefit not just wildlife but the millions of people who hardly ever get a chance to encounter wild animals. One of the tragedies of so many cities and suburbs in North America is that they were put where there was an unusually diverse natural habitat. People were drawn to these sites, but often have managed to destroy them. Thus we have developments named Oak Grove with not an oak in sight and former wetlands rich in species that are now lawns and paved roads. It need not be this way. While people do need places to live, there are models for coexistence that result in better lives for all the inhabitants than what we have now.

We cannot recreate the amazing diversity of plant and animal communities that once lived throughout North America, but we can aim our efforts at creating locally adapted combinations that will be home to wildlife and people. Homeowners of all kinds, along with urban dwellers in condominiums who control their common lands, can make an enormous difference in land available to wildlife. A group of people with adjacent lands who pool their efforts, perhaps agreeing to plant trees along common boundaries, can transform whole city blocks into miniature forests. Joined together with other such groups, their plantings will create corridors for animals, safe havens to live in and to move from one park or open area to another.

Rivers and even smaller streams are especially important links to protect. The important part is to think of links with larger patterns, and to work with urban forestry people, planning commissions, nature centers and others interested in habitat for wildlife.

Corporate properties in cities and suburbs can be part of the wildlife network. There is no rule that says they must remove all trees, choose the best agricultural land, and cover acres with turf and cement. Some years ago I had the good fortune to visit the corporate headquarters of Southern Progress Corporation in Birmingham, a great example of a wildlife-friendly solution. As Linda Askey, garden editor of *Southern Living* magazine, explained, the building was put on the least usable part of the sloping land, and instead of one large flat parking lot, there are several smaller ones built into the hillsides with steps to the building above. Native stands of oak and long-leaf pine were left, and supplemented with Asian species adapted to the area. Fragrant shrubs greet visitors and employees along the entrance walk.

Although not planned specifically for wildlife, it is a haven for many native species. A pair of pileated woodpeckers spend a lot of time in the woods, as does a hawk. When owls perch on tree limbs right outside some of the offices, people call each other to come and watch them. A sycamore outside Linda's office has a small natural cavity that fills with rainwater; she sees

Whether they are at home, at the workplace, at school or in parks, wildlife gardens help people learn ways to live creatively with other animals.

HOW TO RAISE A MONARCH

Betsy Cas in Milwaukee, Wisconsin, has a small urban garden in which she allows milkweed (for monarch butterflies) and dill (for black swallowtails) to grow freely among her flowers. One year she noticed wasps were destroying large numbers of caterpillars so she decided to give the butterflies a little help.

"If I see monarch eggs (easy to identify—white, cone-shaped, on the bottom of milkweed leaves), or tiny, newly hatched caterpillars, I pick a stem of milkweed with the host leaves attached and put it in a shady place in the house. When they look as if they are ready to wander, each caterpillar gets its own quart mason jar. The lids have holes in them with wires attached for later. Keep the jar out of the sun. Every day, without fail, a fresh milkweed leaf must be put in the jar. I toss out the previous day's remnant and dump out the stuff in the bottom of the jar daily. It is quite an operation—but they're my only house pets, and they're temporary at that."

"The caterpillar will suspend its chrysalis from the jar lid. Then I simply unscrew it and hang it in a safe spot outdoors to 'hatch' its monarch, using the wires attached earlier. Often I hang it for a while from the chandelier—the chrysalis is light green with dots of gold—and take it outside when it's almost finished transforming. When the butterfly emerges, it hangs below the empty chrysalis as its wings unfold and dry. It is essential that it have enough room to do this."

The timing is as follows. Eggs are laid, caterpillar emerges in 4 to 8 days. Caterpillar goes into chrysalis 12 to 14 days later. Butterfly emerges 10 to 14 days after that.

Raising a monarch is its own process of discovery, akin to the larger version of discovery you go through in creating an entire wildlife garden.

birds coming to drink from it all day. One year a rabbit raised a family near the picnic table, in a nest among the pine straw under the native rhododendrons. When a pond was put in, ducks arrived to nest before nest boxes went up for them.

That's the kind of work environment and example of ethical land use that NWF is hoping for in promoting its corporate landscaping project. This project, along with another to encourage wildlife gardening at schools, has the potential to transform how people landscape.

Start Children Young

Schools are a great place to extend the concepts of wildlife gardening. In Oklahoma, parent Virginia Kincaid planted a butterfly garden—an outdoor classroom of sorts. Fourth and fifth graders meet regularly as members of the butterfly club, give tours of the garden, can identify most of the 60 species and collect seeds. They also helped campaign to have the black swallowtail designated the official state butterfly, and have received many awards and a lot of publicity for their project.

Other programs in schools use computer technology, like the Journey North program started by Elizabeth Donnelly. Thousands of children a day have tracked 15 migratory bird species, learning ecological lessons about their world.

A Process of Discovery

A distinct palette of American gardens is emerging, complete with animals seen nowhere else on earth. We have here in North America a remarkably diverse number of ecosystems. We also have animal species with adaptations as interesting and varied as those from distant lands and featured on nature programs every week. We just need eyes to see them all, and places where they can live.

One winter I lived in a rented house on Lake Champlain, in Vermont. From October to May is not exactly good gardening weather there. In fact, much of the time the ground is covered in snow. Yet my memories of the garden around that house are full of life: migrating birds in fall, geese honking overhead; tracks of rabbits and squirrels in the snow; chickadees and nuthatches at feeders and on maple branches; early spring frogs "peeping" in the leaf-filled ditch; cardinals in the shrubs and always the squirrels digging in the flower beds.

Wildlife gardening is a way of thinking that has implications well beyond the garden. It requires humility and a willingness to share the land.

For inspiration, we can look to European examples like the hedgerow, and to Native American practices like the burning of grasslands and putting up gourds for purple martins, to new garden techniques like xeriscaping that benefit species adapted to dry regions. Even new technologies like liners for small artificial ponds, to replace those lost to development, make a difference. The goal is a new version of something quite old—a sustainable, comfortable landscape for humans and wildlife.

RESOURCES

ASSOCIATIONS

Birds

American Birding Association
PO Box 6599
Colorado Springs, Colorado 80934
719/578-1614
www.americanbirding.com

Butterflies

Butterfly Lovers International
268 Bush Street
San Francisco, California 94104
415/864-1169

International Federation of Butterfly Enthusiasts
109 Sundown Court
Chehalis, Washington 98532
360/748-4800
www.ifbe.org

North American Butterfly Association
4 Delaware Road
Morristown, New Jersey 07960
973/285-0907

Gardening

American Community Gardening Association
100 North 20th Street
Fifth Floor
Philadelphia, Pennsylvania 19103
215/988-8785

American Horticultural Society
7931 East Boulevard Drive
Alexandria, Virginia 22308
800/777-7931

National Council of State Garden Clubs
4401 Magnolia Avenue
St. Louis, Missouri 63110
314/776-7574

Gardeners of America
PO Box 241
5560 Merle Hay Road
Johnston, Iowa 50131
515/278-0295

Insects

American Entomological Society
Academy of Natural Sciences of
   Philadelphia
1900 Benjamin Franklin Parkway
Philadelphia, Pennsylvania 19103
215/561-3978

Entomological Society of America
9301 Annapolis Road
Lanham, Maryland 20706
301/731-4535

Nature/Conservation

National Audubon Society
700 Broadway
New York, New York 10003
212/979-3000
www.audubon.org

National Wildlife Federation
8925 Leesburg Pike
Vienna, Virginia 22184
703/790-4000
www.nwf.org

Nature Conservancy
1815 North Lynn Street
Arlington, Virginia 22209
800/628-6860
www.tnc.org

CATALOGS

Birding

Duncraft, Inc.
PO Box 9020
Penacook, New Hampshire 03303
800/763-7878

Wild Bird Supplies
4815 North Oak Street
Crystal Lake, Illinois 60012
815/455-4020

Gardening

Bear Creek Corp.
2518 South Pacific Highway
Medford, Oregon 97501
800/278-7673

Bluestone Perennials
7211 Middle Ridge Road
Madison, Ohio 44057
800/852-5243

Cook's Garden
PO Box 535
Londonderry, Vermont 05148
800/457-9703

Dutch Gardens
PO Box 200
Philadelphia, New Jersey 07710
800/818-3861

Edible Landscaping
PO Box 77
361 Spirit Ridge Lane
Afton, Virginia 22920
800/524-4156

Gurney's Seed & Nursery Co.
100 Capital Street
Yankton, South Dakota 57078
605/665-4451

Hilton Co., Inc.
PO Box 1
Graniteville, South Carolina 29829
803/663-9771

J. W. Jung Seed Co.
335 South High Street
Randolph, Wisconsin 53956
800/247-5864

Liberty Seed Co.
461 Robinson Drive Southeast
New Philadelphia, Ohio 44663
330/364-1611

Mellinger's Inc.
2310 West South Range Road
North Lima, Ohio 44452
800/321-7444

Orol Ledden & Sons
Center Avenue
Sewell, New Jersey 08080
800/360-7333

Shepherd's Garden Seeds
30 Irene Street
Torrington, CT 06790
860/482-3638

Spring Hill Nurseries & Breck's Dutch Bulbs
6523 North Galena Road
Peoria, Illinois 61632
800/582-8527

Stark Bro's Nurseries & Orchards Co.
Highway 54 West
Dept. AB1611A7
Louisiana, Missouri 63353
573/754-5511

Thompson & Morgan, Inc.
PO Box 1308
Farraday & Gramme
Jackson, New Jersey 08527
908/363-2225

W. Atlee Burpee & Co.
300 Park Avenue
Warminster, Pennsylvania 18974
800/888-1447

Wayside Gardens
1 Garden Lane
Hodges, South Carolina 29303
800/845-1124

FIELD GUIDES

Stokes Backyard Nature Books
Stokes Nature Guides
Little, Brown & Company
34 Beacon Street
Boston, Massachusetts 02108
617/227-0730

Golden Field Guides
Goldencraft Field Guides
Western Publishing Company, Inc.
1220 Mound Avenue
Racine, Wisconsin 53404
414/633-2431

National Audubon Society Pocket Guides
Alfred A. Knopf, Inc.
201 East 50th Street
New York, New York 10022
212/751-2600

Peterson Field Guides
Houghton Mifflin Company
222 Berkeley Street
Boston, Massachusetts 02116
617/351-5000

WEB SITES

Birding

Birder Home Page
http://www.birder.com

Birdnet: The Ornithological Information Source
http://www.nmnh.si.edu/birdnet/index.html

Butterflies

Butterfly WebSite
http://butterflywebsite.com/

Gardening

Gardening.Com
http://www.gardening.com

Natural Resources Departments

Alabama
  http://www.dcnr.state.al.us/agfd/

Alaska http://www.dnr.state.ak.us/

California
  http://www.state.ca.us/s/natres/

Colorado http://www.dnr.state.co.us/

Delaware
  http://www.dnrec.state.de.us/

Georgia http://www.dnr.state.ga.us/

Illinois http://dnr.state.il.us/

Indiana http://www.ai.org/dnr/

Iowa http://www.state.ia.us/government/dnr/

Louisiana
  http://www.dnr.state.la.us/index.ssi

Maryland
  http://www.gacc.com/dnr/

Michigan
  http://www.dnr.state.mi.us/

Minnesota
  http://www.dnr.state.mn.us/

Missouri
  http://www.state.mo.us/dnr/homednr.htm

Nebraska
  http://www.nrc.state.ne.us/

Ohio http://www.dnr.state.oh.us/

South Carolina
  http://water.dnr.state.sc.us/

South Dakota
  http://www.state.sd.us/state/executive/denr/denr.html

Washington
  http://www.wa.gov/environ.htm

Wisconsin
  http://www.dnr.state.wi.us/

INDEX

A

Acacias, 97, 120
Acraea moth, 44
Alpine meadows, 108
American beautyberry, 107
American goldfinch, 116
American holly, 107
American toads, 13, 39
Amphibians, 21, 38,39
  food for, 39
  reproduction of, 39
  shelter for, 39
Animals
  as gardeners, 47
  as house intruders, 140,41
    tolerance for variety of, 13
Annual rye, 91
Anoles, 40
Antique roses, 107
Aphids, 46
Armadillos, 23, 35, 36, 139
Arthropods, 49
Asters, 99, 127
Australian pine, 92
Azaleas, 96

B

Bailey, Robert G., 22
Barberry, 65
Barred owl, 28
Barrel cactus, 119, 120
Basking turtles, 43
Bats, 36, 37, 138, 140, 141
Bee balm, 99, 107
Bee guards, 126
Bees, 46, 48, 126
Beetles, 44,45
Binoculars, 146
Biophilia hypothesis, 5
Birch groves, 58, 59, 63
Birdbaths, 55, 73, 74, 117, 123, 145
  checking, 74
  choosing, 74
  heated, 76
  placing, 74
Bird feeders, 54, 114,15, 124
  choosing, 124
  squirrels at, 120, 133, 135
Birds, 21, 25,31, 114,15
  feeding, 25,26

houses for, 123
migration of, 115
nesting boxes for, 54
plants for attracting
  in the northeast, 116
  in the pacific region, 122
  in the southeast, 121
  in the southwest, 120
protecting, 66
  protecting plants from, 138
Blackberries, 96
Blackbirds, 7, 11, 83, 119
Black-capped chickadee, 25
Black-footed ferrets, 23
Black swallowtail caterpillar, 45
Blinds, 146
Blueberries, 121, 122
Bluebirds, 26, 27, 30,31, 116, 117
  nesting boxes for, 23
Blue heron, 9
Bluejays, 73, 116, 124
Bog ponds, 79,80
Bogs, 72
Bohemian waxwings, 27,28
Bottom walkers, 43
Box turtles, 43
Bramble fruits, 96
Brambles, 117
Brazilian pepper, 92
Brittlebush, 120
Brown thrashers, 28
Brush piles, 54
Buckthorn, 107
Buckwheat, 91
Bug box, 147
Bullfrogs, 38, 39
Bumblebees, 48
Buntings, 26
Bursage, 120
Bush honeysuckle spirea, 82
Bushtits, 123
Butterflies, 8, 11, 45,46, 82, 127,28, 134, 144
  feeders for, 127
  houses for, 127
  Monarch, 45, 150
  watching, 144
Butterfly bushes, 21, 82
Butternut trees, 116,17

C

Cactus wrens, 27
California ground squirrels, 32, 33
California oak woodlands, 23
Cardinals, 11, 25, 26, 29, 30, 114, 116, 124
Carnivores, 34
Carolina buckthorn, 107
Carolina chickadee, 27
Cas, Betsy, 150
Catbirds, 28
Caterpillars, 45
Cats as danger to wildlife, 66
Cattails, 83
Cedar waxwings, 16, 27,28
Centipedes, 49
Cherries, 121
Chickadees, 11, 25, 27, 29, 30, 73, 117, 124
Children, learning from, 147
Chimney swift, 10
Chinaberry trees, 65
Chipmunks, 33, 73, 117, 132,33, 145
Cholla, 119
Christmas ferns, 103
Chuckwalla, 40
Cicadas, 46
Coexistence, 149,50
Colorado potato beetles, 44
Composites, 99
Coneflower, 99, 107
Conifers, 30, 94
Connections in wildlife gardens, 14
Copperheads, 41
Coral snakes, 41
Coreopsis, 88
Corn and raccoons, 137
Cottonmouths, 41
Crabapples, 95, 107, 122
Crabgrass, 102
Cranberry, 97
Creasy, Rosalind, 140
Creosote, 120
Crossbills, 26
Crows, 26
Cucumber beetles, 44

D

Daisies, 127

C (right column continued)

Deers, 32, 35, 36
  damage caused by, 136,37
  repellents for, 136
Desert regions, 118,20
Desert willow, 120
Diboll, Neil, 108,11
Dill, 99
Diversity in wildlife gardens, 13, 58,59
Dogs as danger to wildlife, 66
Dogwood, 60, 64, 107
Donnelly, Elizabeth, 150
Doves, 119, 124
Downy woodpeckers, 25, 116
Dragonfly, 48
Dung beetles, 44,45
Dutchman's pipe, 101
Dye, John, 73, 127
Dye, Margaret, 73, 127
Dynamic system, forest as, 60

E

Earthworms, 49
Eastern black swallowtail, 109
Eastern bluebirds, 27
Eastern chipmunk, 33
Eastern tiger swallowtail, 69
Eastern woodlands, 23
Echinaceae, 98
Ecological gardening, 148,49
Ecoregions, 22,23
  learning about, 63
Ecosystems, 14
  trees as, 55
Endangered species, 23
English ivy, 100
Ethics in wildlife gardens, 15

F

Fence lizards, 67
Fennel, 99
Ferns, 103
Ferrets, 23
Field guides, 145,46
Finches, 25, 26, 29, 119, 124
Flickers, 29, 30, 119

Flowering cherries, 121
Flowers, 98,99
    composites, 99
    constant bloom in, 99
    mints, 99
Fluharty, Debbie, 85
Flying squirrel, 32
Fontenot, Bill, 107, 121, 149
Food
    for amphibians, 39
    for birds, 25,26
    for hummingbirds, 29
    in wildlife gardens, 54
Forest. See also Trees
    as dynamic system, 60
Fork-tailed bush katydid, 49
Foxes, 34,35
Fox squirrels, 32
Frogs, 38, 39, 145

G

Gaillardia, 99
Garden diary, 147
Garter snakes, 41
Gazebos, 68, 147
Gila monster, 40
Gila woodpeckers, 118, 120
Golden crowned kinglet, 30
Goldenrod, 11, 83, 98
Goldfinches, 26, 29, 62, 73, 116, 119, 124
Gooseberries, 97
Gopher snakes, 41
Gopher tortoises, 43
Grapevines, 101, 116
Grasses
    native, 57, 102
    standard, 102
    in wildlife gardens, 102
Gray squirrels, 4, 21, 32
Great grey owl, 10
Green darner, 49
Green frogs, 39
Grosbeaks, 26, 29, 116, 124
Groundcovers, 57
    in wildlife gardens, 103
Ground squirrels, 32
Growth cycle, completing, 47

H

Habitat gardening, 10
Hackberry, 107
Hairy woodpeckers, 116

Handlenses, 147
Hardiness zones, 22
Hares, 33,34. See also Rabbits
Havahart traps, 137
Hawks, 28,29
Heated bird bath, 76
Hedgerows, 13, 63
    managing, 107
    in wildlife gardens, 107
Herbicides, 56
Heron, 9
Hibiscus, 125
Hognose snakes, 41
Holly, 107, 121
Honeybees, 46
Honeysuckles, 65, 100, 122
Hop vine, 134
Hornets, 49
House, animal intruders in, 140,41
House finches, 26, 119
House mouse, 33
House sparrows, 11, 23, 29
Huckleberries, 121, 122
Hummingbirds, 8, 11, 19,21, 29, 119, 120
    feeders for, 116, 125,26
    food for, 29
    garden for, 125,26
    nesting for, 30,31
    shelter for, 29,30
    water for, 31

I

Indian cherry, 107
Insecticides, 14, 134
Insects, 21, 44,46, 48,49, 121
    controlling, 14, 134
Invasives, avoiding, 65
    in wildlife gardens, 65
Invertebrates, 21, 44,46, 48,49
Island bed in wildlife gardens, 106
Island plantings, 56

J

Japanese barberry, 65
Javelina, 35
Jewelweed, 11, 83
Joe Pye weed, 82, 107

Joshua tree, 120
Journey North program, 150
Juncos, 124

K

Kangaroo mice, 33
Katydid, 49
Kestrels, 28, 116
Kildeer, 118, 119
Kincaid, Virginia, 150
Kinglet, 30
King snakes, 41
Kirkland, A. H., 42

L

Ladybird beetles, 44
Ladybug, 46
Lamium, 103
Lantana, 107
Lavender, 99
Lawn, 56,57
    alternatives to, 87,88
Legal considerations, 87,88
Leopard frog, 38
Liatris, 83
Life cycles, 11
Lightning bugs, 6
Lilacs, 96, 127
Live oaks, 93
Lizards, 40,41, 67, 145
Locust, 46

M

Mahonia, 122
Maidenhair ferns, 103
Mallard ducks, 31
Mammals, 21, 32,37
    browsing, 136
    interaction with humans, 36
    shelter for, 36
    water for, 36
Maples, 23
Marigold, 82
Marshes, 72
Marsh marigold, 82
Meadowlarks, 119
Meadows, 61, 108,11
    maintaining, 109
    starting, 109
    wildflower, 59
Melaleuca, 92
Mescal bean tree, 120
Mesquite, 120
Mexican bean beetles, 44
Mexican redbud, 120
Mexican sunflower, 82
Mice, 33
Microclimates, 13
Midwest, specialty gardens in, 116,17

Milk snakes, 41
Milkweeds, 45, 109, 134
Mints, 99
Mockingbirds, 28, 119
Moles, 33
    fighting, 139
Monarch butterflies, 45
    raising, 150
Moonflower, 69
Moose, 32
Morning dove, 31
Mosquitoes, 81
Mosquito fish, 81
Mosses, 57
Moths, 44, 45,46
Mouth toads, 39
Moving water, creating, 75
Mulberries, 96, 97
Mullein, 117
Multiflora, 65

N

Nardozzi, Barbara, 8,9, 52, 57, 68, 134, 147
Nardozzi, Charlie, 68, 147
Nardozzi, Elena, 147
National Wildlife Federation, 52, 122
    Backyard Wildlife Habitat Program, 5
Native grasses, 57
Native plants
    adding, 64
Natural plants, 63
Neatness standards, relaxing, 62
Nesting boxes, 117, 119,20, 123
Nettles, 45
Newts, 39
Niger, 124
Northeast
    bird plants in, 116
    wildlife gardens in, 116,17
Northern cardinal, 26
Northern oriole, 30
Norway maples, 23
Norway rat, 33
Nuthatches, 11, 25, 27, 29, 30, 114, 124

O

Oaks, 93, 94
Observing, art of, 144
Ocotillo, 119, 120
Ocotillo-saguro, 119
Opossums, 35, 138, 140
Orioles, 30

Otto, Laurie, 87, 148
Owls, 10, 25, 28, 29

P

Pacific gray squirrels, 32
Pacific northwest
  plants for attracting
  birds in, 122
    specialty gardens in,
    122,23
Pacific tree frogs, 39
Palo verde, 120
Pansy, 99
Parasitoids, 48
Parren, Steve, 43, 52, 53,
  64, 90, 100,101, 106,
  107, 116,17, 124, 132,33
Passerine group, 26
Paths, 67
Peepers, 38
Penelle, Barbara, 118,20
Perching group, 26
Perennial beds in wildlife
  gardens, 105
Pesticides, 14, 29, 66
Pests
  controlling, 47
  digging and burrowing,
  139
Pets as danger to wildlife,
  66
Phlox, 109
Physical barriers, 133, 134
Pickerelweed, 82
Pileated woodpeckers, 28
Pine, 92, 94
Pine siskins, 124
Pit vipers, 41
Plant bed, creating, 86
Planting patterns in
  wildlife gardens, 104
Plants
  for attracting birds
    in the northeast, 116
    in the pacific region,
    122
    in the southeast, 121
    in the southwest, 120
  pondside, 82
  water, 83
Pocket gophers, 33, 139
Poison ivy, 101
Poison oak, 101
Poisonous snakes, 140
Ponds, 71, 77,78
  bog, 79,80
  flexible liners for, 78
  installing, 78
  larger, 82
  placing, 78
Pondside plants, 82

Prairie gardening, 87
Prairies, 61, 108,11
  maintaining, 109
  starting, 109
Praying mantis, 48, 49
Predators, 29,30
Prickly pear, 97, 118, 120
Protective coloring, 38
Pruning, 47, 62
Purple coneflower, 99, 107
Purple finches, 26
Purple martins, 27, 31
  building house for, 31
Pyracantha, 82

Q

Quail, 124
Queen Anne's Lace, 23,
  64, 99, 109

R

Rabbitbrush, 120
Rabbits, 7, 9, 33,34
  damage caused by, 137
Rabies, 36, 37, 138
Raccoons, 34, 35, 36, 131,
  140, 141, 145
  and corn, 137
Racerunners, 40
Rappaport, Brett, 148
Raptors, 28,29
Rats, 33
Rat snakes, 41
Rattlesnakes, 41
Red-breasted nuthatches,
  30
Redbud, 120
Red cockaded woodpecker,
  23
Red crested kinglet, 123
Red fox, 35
Redpolls, 124
Red-spotted newt, 39
Red squirrels, 4, 32
Red-winged blackbirds, 7,
  11, 83, 119
Reforestation, 64
Regional focus for wildlife
  gardening, 12
Reproduction of amphib-
  ians, 39
Reproductive cycles, 11
Reptiles, 21, 38, 40,41, 43
Resources, 151,53
Ringtails, 34
Roadrunner, 29
Robins, 27
Rockpiles, 67
Rodents, 33

Rose-breasted grosbeaks,
  26, 116
Rosemary, 99
Roses, 96, 107
Rough-leaved dogwood,
  107
Rudbeckia, 88, 98, 99
Russian olive, 107
Rye, 91

S

Sagebrush, 97
Saguaro, 120
Salamanders, 38, 39
Saltbush, 97
Salvia greggii, 120
Salvias, 99
Sapsuckers, 28, 30
Sassafras, 107
Scarlet tanager, 28
Seeds, planting, 47
Self-heal, 99
Shelter
  for amphibians, 39
  for mammals, 36
  and nesting sites, 54
  in wildlife gardens, 54
Shrews, 32, 33
Shrubs, 60, 91, 121
  in wildlife garden, 96,97
Sitting still, 145
Skunks, 34, 36, 139, 140
Snags, 54
Snakes, 40, 41, 140
Snapping turtles, 43
Snowberries, 97, 107
Snowy owl, 29
Softshells, 43
Soil, preparing, 47
Song-sparrow, 7, 144
Sonoran Desert region, 32
Sounds, night, 145
Southeast
  plants for attracting
  birds in, 121
    specialty gardens in,
    121
Southern alligator lizard,
  40
Southwest
  plants for attracting
  birds in, 120
    specialty gardens in, 8,
    120
Spadefoot toads, 39
Sparrows, 11, 23, 25, 29,
  119, 124
Specialty gardens, 113,30
  in northeast and mid-
  west, 116,17

  in pacific northwest,
  122,23
  in southeast, 121
  in southwest, 118,20
Spicebush, 82
Spiders, 7, 14, 48, 49
Spoo, Alfred J., 79, 82
Spotted tiger moth, 46
Spring azure butterfly, 46
Squash beetles, 44
Squirrels, 4, 21, 32,33,
  139, 140
  at bird feeders, 120,
  133, 135
Starlings, 23, 29, 119
Stein, Sara, 148
Stellar jay, 26
Stone walls, 67
Succession, natural cycles
  of, 111
Suet, 124
Suet feeder, 123
Sumac, 117
Sumac fruits, 97
Sunflowers, 82, 98, 99,
  122
Swallows, 27, 31, 123
Swallowtail, 69, 109
Swallowtail butterfly, 44
Swamp dogwood, 107
Swamps, 72
Sweet woodruff, 103

T

Tanagers, 26, 28
Thorny rose bush, 97
Thrashers, 28
Thrush, 27
Timing, 144
Titmouse, 9, 26,27
Toads, 13, 38, 39, 42, 145
  homes for, 54
Tolerance for variety of
  animal species, 13
Tomato hornworms, 45, 48
Tortoises, 43
Townsend's squirrel, 32
Trap crops, 134
Tree guards, 137,38
Trees, 91
  as ecosystems, 55
  large, 94
  selecting species, 94
  smaller, 95
Tree squirrels, 32
Tree swallows, 123
True bugs, 46
Trumpet creeper, 101
Tularemia, 36
Turtles, 40, 43
Tuttle, Merlin, 37

V

Valley oaks, 93
Verdins, 119
Viburnum, 101
Vines, 60
    choosing, 100,101
    in wildlife garden,
    100,101
Virginia creeper, 100, 101
Voles, 33

W

Warblers, 26, 29, 30
Wasps, 46, 48, 126
Water, 13
    adding to wildlife gar-
    dens, 55
    creating moving, 75
    for mammals, 36
    providing for birds, 115
    quality and mainte-
    nance, 81
    in wildlife gardens,
    71,83
Waterfalls, 78
Waterlilies, 83
Water moccasins, 41
Water plants, 83
Water tables, 72
Waxwings, 16, 27,28, 29
Weasels, 34
Western meadowlarks, 119
Western toads, 39
Wetlands, 71,72
Whiptails, 40
White breasted nuthatch-
    es, 25
White oaks, 93
Wildflower meadow, 59
Wild ginger, 103
Wildlife gardens
    connections in, 14
    diversity in, 13
    enjoying, 143,50
    ethics in, 15
    evaluating plants for, 93
    flowers in, 98,99
    food and shelter in, 54
    grasses in, 102
    groundcovers in, 103
    as habitat, 10,11
    hedgerow in, 107
    as human habitat, 53
    island bed in, 106
    overall design for, 90
    perennial beds in, 105
    planting patterns in,
    104

plantings in, 85,111
reasons for creating, 3,7
regional focus in, 12
renovating existing, 92
shrubs in, 96,97
specialty, 113,30
starting from scratch, 91
strategies for, 51,69
    adding native plants,
    64
    avoiding invasives, 65
    creating places to
enjoy, 68,69
    diversity in, 58,59
    learning about ecore-
gions, 63
    looking at present
plants, 52
    minimizing pesticides, 66
    planning head, 52
    protecting your, 66
    relaxing neatness stan-
dards, 62
    rethinking lawn in,
55,57
    stone walls, rock piles,
fences and paths in, 67
    water access in, 55
    trees in, 94,95
    vines in, 100,101
    water in, 71,83
    wildlife as problem in,
131,41
"Wild Ones, The," 148
Wild peccary, 35
Wild roses, 96
Wilson, Ann, 122
Wilson, E. O., 5
Wilson, Eric, 122
Winter, water in, 76
Wintergreen, 103
Wisteria, 68
Woodchucks, 32, 33, 34
    damage caused by, 137
Wood frogs, 39
Woodhouse toads, 39
Woodpeckers, 5, 23, 25,
    28, 29, 30, 36, 116, 118,
    120, 124
Woodpiles, 54
Wrens, 27, 118

Y

Yarrow, 99
Yellow warblers, 26
Yews, 9